Waiting for the Dark,
Waiting for the Light

Ivan Klíma was born in 1931 in Prague, where he now lives, and was editor of the journal of the Czech Writer's Union during the Prague Spring. He is the author of many plays, stories and novels including *The Ultimate Intimacy*, which, along with a collection of stories, *My Golden Trades*, and a non-fiction book, *The Spirit of Prague*, are also available from Granta Books. His work, which is now published worldwide, was banned in his country until just a few years ago.

IVAN KLÍMA

Waiting for the Dark, Waiting for the Light

TRANSLATED FROM THE CZECH
BY PAUL WILSON

Granta Books
London

Granta Publications, 2/3 Hanover Yard, London N1 8BE

First published in Great Britain by Granta Books 1994
This edition published by Granta Books 1998

A CIP catalogue record for this book is
available from the British Library.

1 3 5 7 9 10 8 6 4 2

Printed and bound in Great Britain by Mackays of Chatham PLC

Contents

CHAPTER ONE

1

A CROWD HAD begun to gather at the lower end of the
square. Most of the people were young. Some of them
Pavel remembered from earlier demonstrations. He had a
good memory for faces and even thought he recognized
some of the onlookers lounging on the pavement. Like
him, they were fixtures on these occasions. They were
probably here on duty too, though it was duty of a different
kind. Not far away, in front of a large display window full of
shoes, was a man with a small movie camera. He didn't rec-
ognize the man, though he knew most people in his line of
work; perhaps he was a curious tourist, an amateur photog-
rapher or someone taking pictures of the demonstrators for
the archives of the security police.

But what was he doing here himself? Why were he and
his crew filming these events? For television? The network
wouldn't broadcast a thing he shot, or rather what they did
broadcast would have little to do with what actually hap-
pened. Perhaps he was working for the future.

But what was the future?

The future was a time that called into question every-
thing that came before it.

Several uniformed policemen were standing around on
the pavement. As usual, it was a peaceful demonstration.
No one was shouting slogans, or getting ready to throw

stones through shop windows, overturn cars or attack the police. Yet in most of the faces he observed through his viewfinder, there was tension, the nervous anticipation of the inevitable clash that would take place according to precise, though unwritten and not exactly high-minded, principles.

Why had the demonstrators come? What were they trying to prove, or change? What did they believe in that made them willing to endure being beaten, locked up, dismissed from their jobs? Was their protest for some higher cause, or were they there only because there wasn't enough else to interest or motivate them—were they simply bored?

He wanted to ask them, but knew there was an impenetrable barrier between himself and them, a barrier symbolized by the logo on the transmission van and by his camera, a barrier as blatant as the double row of barbed-wire fencing that isolated this country from its neighbours, or at least from the country to which he had once foolishly attempted to flee. Sometimes he felt a vague uneasiness about being on this side of the barrier yet, at the same time, he felt safe. No one would beat him or interrogate him or try to blow him off the street with a water-cannon.

The crowd closed ranks, although there were still no more than a few hundred people in it. A young woman raised a piece of white cloth above her head. It bore the inscription LESS SMOKE, MORE AIR. He took a shot of the banner, studying the woman's face and hands as he did so.

Her hands were small, almost childlike, with unpainted nails, and they were quivering slightly, perhaps because of the wind straining against the banner. Her face too was childlike, guileless and innocent. For a moment she reminded him of Albina. Where was she and what would she be doing right now? She might be somewhere here on this square holding a sign above her head. He'd put her out of his mind for so long. What would he say to her if she appeared? What would she say to him if she saw him on the pavement, trying to capture her and her presence on an Ampex tape?

She would say: how could you bring yourself to do this? Or she would say nothing at all. Why should she talk to him?

He looked around at the crowd, partly out of professional interest—in case he saw a new banner—but he also wondered if he might not actually catch a glimpse of her. She wasn't here, of course; there were only more uniformed men on the pavement and a lorry with a water-cannon mounted over the cab which had begun moving slowly down from the upper regions of the square. In the same instant the crowd came together and acquired a voice of its own, a low rumble like a swarm of bees or a looming thunderhead. He felt its agitation grow in anticipation of the coming clash.

The clash would be as absurd as all the others before it, but there was no stopping it. Everyone knew this: those who would administer the beatings and those who would be beaten. This utter certainty transformed the raw determination on both sides into movements that almost seemed preordained. Even Pavel found himself hoping that the clash would soon start, not because he was eager for violence, but because he wanted the inevitable to be over with so that he could do his job and leave.

A yellow-and-white car with a large loudspeaker on its roof moved slowly down the square. The amplified voice, sounding more bored than threatening, announced that the gathering was illegal and ordered everyone present to disperse peacefully. The clamour around Pavel grew.

He took a shot of the car with the loudspeaker and then looked back at the woman with the touchingly naïve banner. The white cloth in her hands was trembling more obviously now.

When it was over he walked down one of the narrow side-streets to where he had parked his red sports car. He looked at it, as he always did, with affection, then got in and drove off. The road and the pavements were still wet, and the buildings were spattered with water, but anyone who happened to come this way now would be unaware of what had happened here only moments before. He drove as fast as he dared through the narrow, winding streets. He would love to drive somewhere far away, as far away as possible from people, demonstrations and water-cannons, but he'd promised to visit Eva that evening, and had promised her son that he would stop off at the stadium to watch his game—he was the goalkeeper of a youth soccer team. He was a sweet kid, and Pavel felt a fatherly concern for him. It was certainly more pleasant to demonstrate his interest in the kid by watching a game than by talking to him about school in the evening. First, however, he had to drop in at the studio, look at the tapes and hand over his material.

The news-room secretary told him the boss had asked where he was twice that day. She supposed it was because of the president's birthday. They'd talked about it at the meeting, she said; it was a big event, they were going to have to shoot a special report at the castle, and he and Sokol were naturals for the job.

He didn't respond. It gave him some private satisfaction that they would trust him, of all people, with such a responsible job, but publicly he liked to say that the only thing he had in common with the head of state was that both of them had been let out of prison the same year.

As usual, the small editing room was hot and stuffy and stank of smoke and bad coffee. To make matters worse it was crammed with people who wanted to know what had really happened on the square. Two bottles of wine and some glasses stood on the mixing desk. Someone must have been celebrating something; you could always find something to celebrate. He pulled a banknote out of his wallet, tossed it in the kitty and poured himself a drink, then handed the tape to the executive producer, a churlish man named Halama, who slipped it into the machine.

Pavel watched the monitor intently. There was the young woman who wanted to breathe less smoke and more air, but now he noticed a young man standing near her. He was tall and thin, wearing a check shirt, and had a pale, dreamy face that looked briefly and sullenly into the camera. He has blue eyes like me, Pavel thought. In fact, he's very like me twenty-five years ago. Would I have been out there too, demonstrating, if I were twenty years younger?

The young man moved out of the frame. The car with the loudspeaker crossed the screen. The crowd roared and stood its ground. A squad of riot police with truncheons poured out of one of the side-streets. The crowd began to break up and retreat, chanting: 'Why can't you be human? Why can't you be human?'

'All of that's got to go absolutely!' said Halama irritably. As if the rest of it could stay.

He tried to spot the girl with the banner again and couldn't, but he noticed the young man in the check shirt holding his hands over his face. Truncheons thumped and thudded against bodies; there were shouts and curses. Someone behind him sobbed. He turned around, surprised. Halama's secretary was wiping her eyes. Then she quickly shook her head: 'It's nothing, it's nothing,' she apologized, as though she'd done something inappropriate.

A precisely aimed stream of water came pouring out of the water-cannon. More shouting and running, then a rather good close-up of a face streaming with water, hair drenched, eyes blinded.

Pavel looked at Halama, whose narrow lips were drawn tight, his grey face expressing distaste. Was this a response to what had happened? No: more likely to the fact that it had all been captured so clearly on tape. 'Don't even think of using any of this!' he said.

'Why do they do it?' whispered the secretary behind Pavel.

Her question was not directed at him, but it was one he had asked himself. Only now, when someone else asked it, did an answer occur to him. 'They want something different,' he said.

'But they won't get it that way.'

'Maybe they're not after anything in particular at all.'

He turned back to the monitor. He'd managed to take a wide shot of the fleeing crowd. The retreat was so well executed it looked staged.

Almost thirty years ago he too had wanted something different, wanted it so badly he had tried to escape from the country. It wasn't that they'd gone after him with truncheons, like this. Back then, it would have been futile to demonstrate; no one would have turned up. Why had he tried to get out? It was a question he still found hard to answer. Perhaps because his father had left his mother and he couldn't stand living in a half-empty house. He had also wanted to travel. To see Indians, the Yucatán and the Mayan pyramids. He'd gone to the Mexican embassy and offered to work for them for nothing. They asked him what skills he had. He was good at photography and knew a little Spanish. Unfortunately there are many people like you, they said. If you were a doctor, we might consider you. So he decided to run away, and Peter decided to go with him.

He'd met Peter by chance. They were both taking pictures at the zoo, in the reptile pavilion, when they got talking. Pavel said he'd like to make films about wild animals—lions in the desert, tigers in the jungle, kangaroos in the bush, rattlesnakes or sand vipers sunning themselves on rocks. Peter was more interested in the snake as a symbol. 'The serpent was more subtle than any beast of the field which the Lord God had made,' he said, quoting the Bible. The snake had seduced man into curiosity, made him long for omniscience, and so it had become a symbol of evil and satanic will, though not everywhere and not to everyone. Peter loved to display his knowledge. Some Egyptian pharaohs wore bronze headbands representing a snake, which they believed would protect them from evil. Some African and Indian tribes thought of the snake as a divine being. Peter wanted to study theology. He was fascinated by every facet of the relationship between man and God, by anything which suggested superhuman power. There was something pontifical in his manner of speaking, as though he were always trying urgently to communicate something. His voice was unpleasantly shrill. It would be a handicap were he to become a preacher, but in the conversations he had with Pavel it didn't matter. The important thing was that he too longed to travel, to visit the Holy Land and Rome, Athens, Corinth, Ephesus and the temples in Luxor and Palenque. The very first time they met, they shared their secret wishes and tried to outdo each other with their knowledge. But neither of them had the slightest hope of seeing what they longed to see, or even of getting beyond the border, for the border was sealed with barbed wire. The wire was a symbol, like the snake. How could you possibly live your entire life, learn anything, or achieve anything in a country fenced in with barbed wire?

They began to fashion plans to escape. At first it was a game, but gradually they surrendered to the allure of their own longings, those perfectly integrated steps that would take them to their goal. Who had been the instigator of this act that had changed the course of both their lives? He was the more pragmatic and had far more practical ideas. But he also had greater misgivings. Peter was more casual, and besides, he firmly believed, sacrilegiously perhaps, given the implications of what they were preparing to do, that the mercy and love of God would protect them. Peter had turned out to be wrong about divine protection, but his faith had made Pavel start to believe in something as well.

What had he actually believed in then?

That you must not live without purpose, that you must look to the consequences of your actions, live in a way that brings harm or pain to no one. And you must leave some trace of yourself behind, and that trace would be a work of art. At the time he hadn't been entirely sure what form it would take, but he knew he had the power to create it.

The final escape plan seemed brilliantly simple. They would cross the border in the north where there was no barbed wire, continue to the sea, then catch a boat. Stowing away seemed easier than cutting through wire, clambering over a wall or swimming across a heavily patrolled river. Unfortunately it wasn't as easy as they'd imagined. The God Peter thought of as their protector was clearly preoccupied with worries of cosmic dimensions in which the two of them had no place.

The tape was nearly over. All that remained at the scene were the victors, puddles of water and several men looking on from the pavement with professional interest. Pavel tried to fix their faces in his memory. Why? Just in case.

Halama stood up disdainfully. Someone behind him began to clap, and several others joined in. Were they applauding his professional achievement, the victors, the puddles of water or the enemy that had just been dissipated?

All of us applaud on demand, yet we fear everyone.

2

THE BOY WAS wearing a black jersey and yellow gym shorts—the colours of a jaguar. A proper goalkeeper's outfit. He was tall for his age but still too short to block a shot placed just below the crossbar.

Pavel stood behind the goal and asked him how they were doing.

'OK, but I've been lucky. They hit the post.' The boy gestured to his right. 'I still haven't had a touch. It's good you've come, Pavel. I never know when to move forward.'

'You have to make up your mind fast. When a sheep or a wild boar starts day-dreaming, it misses the right moment to run away, and the jaguar gets it.' He felt awkward with the boy; he was really talking about his own experience with Peter.

The play moved closer to the goal, and he was glad not to have to talk. When had he ever been able to act quickly, with resolve? They'd caught him once and locked him up, and since then he'd simply tried to keep out of their way. An animal might seem to know when his life or his freedom is threatened, but do people? They think they're running towards freedom when in fact they're rushing headlong into a trap.

'Now! Now!' he shouted at the boy in the black-and-yellow outfit. The boy charged out to meet the attacking players, managed to get to the ball and deflect it off his fist back into the field. He stood for a while at the edge of the box and looked at the retreating cluster of players.

'How was that?' he said when he came back.

'That was great, Robin, you got to the ball first.'

'I need you to stand there all the time and tell me when to move out,' said the boy.

He wanted to tell him that that would only ruin him as a goalie, but he stopped himself.

How old would his own son have been today? If indeed it had been a boy. Whenever he thought about the child, he thought about him as a son. How would he have treated him? Would he have been a good father?

I'd probably have done a decent job, he thought. I take this one out in my car and I advise him when to go for the ball. But I know that I can walk out on his mother and him any time I like, without losing any sleep over it. The truth is he's not my own son and he never will be, and his mother will probably never be my wife.

After the match he waited for the boy to shower and change. When they got in the car he noticed a cheap gold ring glittering on Robin's finger. It didn't go with his jeans at all. Eva must have got it for him. That was her business, their business. He never asked about more than he absolutely needed to know.

Eva lived on the seventh floor of a tower block. The flat had one large room and two smaller ones. Her former husband lived in the larger of these. He was a quiet, affable person, who worked as a fitter and was away from home most of the time on construction jobs. He could probably have found himself a new flat but didn't appear to be looking for one. With this arrangement, he was at least close to his son, and perhaps he wanted to stay close to his former wife as well.

She never told him why her marriage was over. He assumed it was because her husband did not seem prosperous or important enough. Pavel was a better bet in her eyes; prosperity, like importance, is all too relative. Eva had sought him out herself. Two years ago she had seen a film he'd made on divorce and its impact on children, and she had written to him about it. She was in a similar situation and wanted to see him and ask his advice.

The film was a documentary he'd directed and appeared in. The problem it dealt with had haunted him ever since his own childhood, and he was pleased that the film had spoken to someone. He wrote back, giving his home address. Several days later she rang his doorbell. It was evening. She introduced herself and asked hesitantly if she was disturbing him or his wife. She was wearing a short bluish-purple skirt, a reddish-purple sweater, high dark purple leather boots and an ultramarine ribbon in her dyed-red hair. Large green jasper earrings were swinging from her ears. He assured her that she wasn't disturbing him, that he wasn't married and that his mother was away. She was clearly pleased to hear this. She walked in without an invitation, her hips swaying and her bracelets clinking with every step. She sat down on a chair facing him, her skirt riding up as she crossed her legs. She looked at him eagerly. He asked what he could do for her. He had done a lot for her already, she said, just by making the film and letting her see him. Without boring him with the banal details, she was living with a man she couldn't respect. She'd married him because she was pregnant; there was no love between them. She had a bizarre way of speaking, hesitating in the middle of sentences, sometimes not completing them. Her face was plain, but there was something bold and inviting in her every movement and glance. When she finished telling her story, she fell silent and seemed to be waiting for him to embrace her. When he didn't, she stood up, walked over to him and said, 'I want you to make love to me.'

When Pavel let himself into Eva's flat, Argus bounded out to meet him, planted his huge paws on his chest and licked his face. Only then did Eva appear, freshly made-up as always, her mouth painted, her eye-shadow replenished, strawberry-blonde hair combed high. She could have gone directly in front of a camera. He had to bend over slightly to kiss her on the mouth. She smiled at him. She did everything she could to bind him to her. She tried to be pleasant, to tolerate his eccentricities, his occasional disappearances, his silences. She even went with him sometimes to visit his mother, always remembering to take flowers, though his mother forgot about her the minute she left. She did his laundry for him, cooked for him, made love to him and listened to what he said. If he was silent for too long, she would complain that he hardly ever spoke to her.

What did they talk about?

About life, of course.

What was life?

Life was a heap of things, an enormous accumulation of old clothes, tubes, creams, mincing-machines, coffee-mills. It was also masses of wires, lamps, mirrors, cameras, cassettes, scissors and water-cannons.

He took his sweater off and went into the living-room.

The television in the corner was on as usual, but nobody was watching. The sound was turned down, and for a while he watched a silent singer swinging her arms to the rhythm, while behind her waves beat against a rock and a gull hovered overhead. Lacklustre, empty images, but who had any good ideas any more? Who had a point of view? Who was doing decent work? He was, or at least he could still inject the most heavy-handed material with life, and one day, when they let him show what he could really do . . .

'Guess what we're having for supper,' said the boy, coming up to him.

He shook his head.

'Fried chicken. Your favourite.'

'I eat everything.'

'Except potato dumplings.'

'Potato dumplings I can do without. They don't fit down my throat.' He made a face as though he were gagging.

The boy laughed. 'Dad likes them.' Then he stopped. 'He was here yesterday,' he said, somewhat embarrassed. 'He bought me these jeans.'

'And the ring?'

'Yeah. Do you like it?'

'Let me see it.' He took the ring from the boy. 'I've never worn rings,' he said, avoiding the question. The ring had a hallmark and might have been a family heirloom. The boy's paternal grandfather had once owned a factory. The factory had been nationalized, but the state had apparently let the family keep their jewellery. Perhaps it was the jewellery that had first attracted Eva to her husband. But either there wasn't enough to go around, or it wasn't enough to compensate for the impoverished heir's other shortcomings.

Pavel had inherited nothing. When they caught him, he was wearing a threadbare duffle-coat with twenty marks in his pocket and some maps in a knapsack: a map of Germany, one of Belgium and a forty-year-old map of Mexico. It was all he could get. What do you need a map of Mexico for around here? I wanted to trade it for a local map. They struck him in the face and told him to stop lying. Still, he held out for several days. They told him there was no point in denying anything, because Peter had already confessed. It seemed likely. Lying went against Peter's nature. In fact, Peter hadn't talked until they'd told him Pavel had confessed. The two of them had fallen for the oldest trick in the book, but they were still young, stupid and inexperienced.

Sometimes, when he thought back over this botched period in his life, he thought that the worst thing about it was not the locked doors, nor the guards shouting at them, nor the fact that there was never enough to eat and what little they had was often stolen from them: it was that everything was saturated with lies. Meanness, rottenness, baseness lay concealed behind every word, every allusion, every promise, every smile. Only later did he come to understand that his time in prison was the best preparation he could have had for the life awaiting him outside. Everyone had to get used to it, and he at least had had a crash course.

The boy left the room. When Eva opened a cupboard to take out the tablecloth, he saw several colourful sweaters in Cellophane wrapping on a shelf. 'What are those?'

'They brought these to the shop yesterday, so I kept some back. They'll certainly sell well. Shetland wool.' She took one of them off the shelf and unwrapped it.

'I know. You've got your own private customers.'

'I have more customers than goods.'

'One day you'll have your own shop and then you won't have to drag these things home.'

'You think so?' She smiled happily as though he'd told her he loved her. She longed for a shop of her own, but the truth was she couldn't possibly imagine it. Most people can't imagine a life that is any different from the one they are actually living. They can dream about it, they can even go into the streets and demonstrate for it, but they still can't imagine what it would be like.

Eva's smile reminded him of the shy smile of Ditta in a film by the Jensens, and it moved him. Maybe he should spend more time with her, be a little nicer to her. She was all he had. As she bent over by the cupboard, he reached out and stroked her hair.

She looked up at him in surprise. 'Is anything the matter?'

'No, nothing—nothing at all. Why?'

She went into the kitchen and after a while came back with supper. His sudden feeling of warmth towards her had, in the meantime, evaporated. She had nothing at all in common with Ditta; there was no shyness in her demeanour. Besides, he was certain she valued success over kindness. Success meant buying cheap and selling dear. It was a simple formula, and kindness or no kindness, he obviously fitted in with it. He knew how to sell his abilities, and himself.

Eva ate only a few mouthfuls. She was afraid of gaining weight, although there was no danger of that. She had a pretty figure, with small breasts, slim hips and a long neck. He'd photographed her nude several times, mostly with her face obscured. Her face looked good behind a counter, but it wouldn't have been right on the cover of a magazine. There was something missing from it, the thing that would make it special, a birthmark, a small scar, a mole. But most of all it lacked interest.

'Looks as though I'm going to have to do a film about the big chief,' he told her.

'That's good, isn't it?'

'I'd rather film animals than people. Big animals. But then again not as big as this particular one. Not as old, either. And certainly not the kind they're likely to send to the slaughterhouse.'

She looked at him in astonishment. She wasn't used to hearing him talk like that. 'Does that mean you're going to turn the job down?'

'They haven't offered it to me yet.' The first time he had been entrusted with filming the president, he had felt honoured. Gaining access at such a high level strengthened his position, made him less vulnerable. And the president's life, which had been so full of ups and downs, was an attractive subject for a film. Yet so much had changed in the past few years. The president's influence was in decline, and so was the position of everyone connected with him. Perhaps the best thing would be to turn down the offer when it came. But what excuses could he make? That he was tired? That he had heart trouble? Perhaps a doctor would back him up. But the idea that the job might go to someone else didn't appeal to him either. Presidents come and presidents go, and the president who replaces the present one will need someone to record his achievements. Whom will he choose? The most skilled and experienced manipulator he can find. No, he mustn't drop out of the game, not even for a second. The single most important thing was to recognize in time that the old game had ended and a new one had begun.

He quickly swallowed a mouthful of food. Whether they offer the job to him or to someone else, those in charge will not allow authentic films. They won't be looking for a genuine, inimitable work of art. 'Did any replies to the ad come?' he asked Eva, changing the subject.

'Yes,' she said happily. 'Do you want to see?'

She longed for a house of her own. She was saving up for it and she assumed he was too. Until then, she was trying at least to exchange this flat for another. Perhaps she believed that once she had a flat all to herself she would have him to herself as well, and that he would finally marry her and surrender his right to leave at any time. He neither confirmed nor denied her belief. He studied the ads, and occasionally the two of them would ring doorbells and look at flats which, fortunately, he could declare too ugly, or which were no longer available. He had no desire whatever to acquire a cage in which he would have to set up house with her.

He picked up the leather folder and leafed through the papers in it.

'Does anything take your fancy?'

He shrugged.

'Kučera came yesterday.' She always referred to her former husband by his last name. 'I don't like running into him all the time.'

'Robin told me he'd been.' Pavel got up from the table, but there was nowhere to go. He'd been coming here for two years and hadn't yet found a corner of the flat he could call his own.

She got up too and stood close to him, waiting for him to embrace her. 'Sometimes I think you don't really want to be with me.'

'I'd never be with anyone I didn't want to be with,' he replied, using a line he'd heard in a television serial. But the reply satisfied her for the moment, or she thought it proper to pretend that it did.

What did it mean to be with someone?

He lit a cigarette and waited. The boy came in to say goodnight. Eva unfolded the sofa bed and went into the bathroom.

He hadn't been with anyone for a long time. At one time he had had a number of friends, but they had drifted away, their places taken by colleagues at work, some of whom kowtowed to him, while others watched, waiting for him to make a mistake so that they could step into his shoes. Until recently, he had occasionally stayed with his mother. But she had suddenly aged and was losing her sense of time and her interest in the world around her. Sometimes she could be unexpectedly and unreasonably hostile. He might pity her, but he could no longer be with her.

He was overwhelmed by restlessness. He wanted to go somewhere, do something, change something. Go back somewhere.

He opened the drinks cabinet. There was always a bottle of cognac there, and a glass just for him. He uncorked the bottle and drank from it.

The bathroom was free. He went in to wash, then tiptoed past the room where the former husband sometimes lived in silence, and slipped into bed beside Eva. He took her in his arms and without a word skilfully caressed her, just as he had done yesterday, and a year ago. Then he placed his palm on her stomach because he knew that she liked that and would fall asleep more quickly. As he did so he looked into the semi-darkness, faintly illuminated by the lights in the street, and into the windows of the tower block opposite. He was afraid he wouldn't fall asleep. Recently he'd been having more and more trouble sleeping. If only he had something to think about, but nothing in his immediate future seemed worth the effort. What was the point of replaying the same old images and the same old stories? He should be inventing new ones. But he was too tired for that now. Whenever he began a new story these days, he tired of it before he had finished.

They sent him to an operating theatre to film a chief surgeon who was about to be awarded a state prize. The surgeon wouldn't allow him to light the room properly: the cables were apparently not sterile. Pavel was so angry he felt like packing everything up and walking out, or at least refusing to operate the camera. But he was fascinated by the hands of the young woman passing the instruments to the surgeon. He wanted to see the face that went with them, but it was hidden behind a mask. Only dark blue melancholy eyes beneath a high forehead were visible; the blue in them was so unusual they seemed foreign.

He asked a man in a white gown what her name was.

'That's Albina,' the man replied.

'A strange name.'

'It suits her.'

How long had it been since she appeared in his life? And how often had he replayed that scene? It didn't matter. Perhaps it would put him to sleep. Autumn. Leaves drifting down on the gatehouse. He almost doesn't recognize her because she's no longer in white. The wind plays with her red skirt. Her wide lips seem sensuous.

'Excuse me, Miss Albina, do you have a moment?'

'How do you know my name? I don't know you.'

'This afternoon in the operating room—I was the one behind the camera.'

'What do you want?'

'Nothing, really.'

'Then don't bother me, I'm in a hurry.'

'Could I walk a little way with you?'

'Thanks, I'm fine by myself.'

'Would you mind if I met you here some day when you're not in a hurry?'

'I'm always in a hurry.'

Some conversations stick in the mind. The first is usually the most memorable, followed by the last. It tends to be the same with facial expressions. She attempted a severe look of rebuff, but it did not change the softness of her features. He watched her as she walked away. She seemed smaller than she really was, as though she had withdrawn into herself. Perhaps it was the cold. Rain had begun to fall, and she was not wearing a coat.

Next day was the last day of filming in the hospital, but she was not on duty. The man who had revealed her name yesterday told him she would be working the night shift.

Next morning he waited for her at the entrance with a bouquet of roses.

Why? He didn't know. Probably out of wounded pride. He didn't like to admit that he'd been rejected.

'I can't accept flowers from you.'

'But I brought them for you.'

'Why?'

'To make you happy.'

'Why would you want me to be happy?'

'Because I find you attractive.'

'I don't like people who work in television.'

'That's discrimination,' he objected.

'I don't like people who work for our television,' she corrected herself. 'Because of what you do, because of the people you make programmes about. Like the surgeon—he's not a good man.'

'Why do you work for him?'

'Because I'm a nurse. I was working in the operating room before he came.'

'Couldn't you have left?'

She was silent for a moment. 'There's a difference. You probably can't feel it. But why should I explain it to you?' She gave a shrug and walked away. He took the flowers to his mother.

A week later he tried again. He left tickets for a concert at the gatehouse along with a card that said: I'd love you to come. But she didn't.

In a few weeks he would be forty-five. What had he actually accomplished? He'd made several short documentaries and a lot of story items that were instantly forgotten. He'd forgotten most of them himself. He had renovated a cottage acquired cheaply from someone who had recently gone into exile (life is full of paradoxes); he'd filled it with things that gave him no particular pleasure. He'd slept with a lot of women but he'd never fathered a child.

Eva was sound asleep, and most of the windows in the other blocks of flats were now dark. He got out of bed, put on his clothes, crept out of the room and left the flat with a feeling of relief.

The streets were like a graveyard. Graveyards remind us of the vanity of all human endeavour. He got into his red Fiat. At night he could drive fast; in half an hour he would be at his cottage.

What would he do there?

He could work on some of his scripts, on some of the screenplays he might one day manage to finish and film. He could give some thought to his future or examine his past.

The image was always the same: a disgusting office that reminded him of an interrogator's room. A personnel manager is leafing through some documents. Most probably they're Pavel's files: a collection of his deeds, his misdeeds, his crimes, fabricated from allegations, catchwords, denunciations and lies. Finally the man raises his bloodshot eyes with dark circles under them. 'So, you want to work in television?'

That had been seventeen years ago. At the time, he had nodded and thus made a decision to join the select few who took the places of those who'd just been fired. He was helping to replace those with whom, until that very moment, he had sympathized.

Yet it didn't feel like a real decision at all; he was simply accepting a job. The position was so menial and unimportant that he could see no reason to refuse. Still, he talked it over with his mother, and with Peter and Alice. His mother thought he should take it. Peter said that he personally would never cross the threshold of that factory of lies. Alice disagreed: she said it depended on what he did there and how he behaved. Everyone had the right to work at what he knows how to do and what he wants to do, even if others have been denied that right. The conditions in which we all live, she said, were not his fault, and he had even tried to escape from them, but it hadn't worked out and as a result his life had been made very difficult for a long time. Alice understood him.

He began work as an assistant cameraman. He dragged

cables around and set up lights as he was directed.

But of course it had been a real decision after all. He believed he would be promoted and eventually make his own programmes, his own films.

He was diligent and patient. He knew that in the end they would let him do what he wanted, and they did, though he had to wait several years.

Fate was on his side. Two young men hijacked a school bus and demanded to be allowed to cross the border. In the twenty years since he had tried to escape, the world had grown used to more extreme methods of breaking through the limits of what was permitted.

The border guards promised the hijackers that they would get what they wanted if they let the children go. The hijackers agreed but, once the children had been released, the border guards reneged. They blocked the bus's passage and opened fire, killing one of the hijackers and the driver.

Pavel discovered that an old classmate of his was one of the guards involved. This prompted him to propose a documentary about the event. His producer granted permission, and his former classmate agreed to meet him—even promising to take him fishing in the border zone.

Almost as soon as he arrived, his classmate gave him fishing tackle and a pair of waders, and they walked along a line of warning signs and through a zone of barbed-wire barriers until they reached a stream that formed the border. Almost twenty years had gone by since his escape attempt, yet every step he took made him tremble.

The stream meandered through a shallow wooded valley, and from this vantage point the wire was invisible. His classmate, who by now had reached the rank of major, stood on a flat stone, threw in his line and, as though they had really got together just to go fishing, began to tell him how hard it was to catch the wily grayling.

Pavel also threw his line in the water but instead of keeping his eye on the float, he looked across the border. For the first time in his life, another country lay within reach, but he no longer yearned to go there and felt merely a sense of curiosity, wondering if a spy, a lost tourist or a border guard might suddenly appear from the other side to find him wading in this stream with the border running down the middle of it.

The major climbed down off the rock and walked downstream. 'Be careful, Pavel,' he said. 'Don't stumble on to the other side. You never know who might be hidden over there behind those fir-trees.'

He nodded. He understood that his uniformed classmate might get into trouble even if he didn't step over the imaginary line. He had brought him here knowing full well that years ago, when Pavel had tried to reach the other side, he'd been caught by body-snatchers wearing the same uniform the major was wearing now. But that was long ago, and now everything had changed. Pavel was here to make a film about him and his heroism. He hoped that when his superiors saw the film on television, they would promote him.

'You come here often?' Pavel asked.

'Every day if I could,' replied his classmate, 'but I can barely make it here once a month. It's worst when the brass pay a visit. I'd bring them here, but they always get drunk, and no one can keep track of them. Besides, they all want to catch a ton of fish, so we've got a special pond, just for them. It's in the border zone too, but before you get to the wire. You just toss in your line and reel in the fish. That's not fishing, it's like shooting them in a barrel.'

'And what about those two hijackers? Wasn't that like shooting fish in a barrel too? I'm sorry, I know you were just doing your duty.'

'It's too bad the driver bought it and not the other bastard. That's what really bothers me.'

'But did it have to happen at all?'

'What do you mean?'

'I'm just asking, before we start. I don't have my camera here and no one will hear us.'

'You think we should have let them go?'

'That's what I'm asking.'

'They had rifles and a busload of kids.'

'But they let the kids go!'

'Once we promised them they could cross the line.'

'That's what I'm getting at—you made a promise.'

'Are you saying we should have kept our word?'

'I'm just asking.'

'If we'd let them go, we'd have had two more attempts within a week, and four more after that. And then one day they wouldn't let the kids go, or someone inside the bus would lose it and let them all have it.'

'I was just asking.' He began to regret coming here, regret letting himself be drawn to this place, and by such an occasion. He was ashamed of himself for not asking tougher questions, for not raising obvious objections. If the borders had been open in the first place, he wouldn't have had to go to jail back then, and no one would have felt compelled to hijack a bus full of children just to get to the other side.

The man in uniform suddenly froze, then abruptly yanked his rod back. In the clear water of the brook Pavel could see a trout, solidly hooked, attempting to wriggle to safety under a nearby boulder. What hope of escape is there when we swallow the hook? And are we even aware that we have?

'They were the ones who started shooting. They blew out the windows·in the guardhouse. And the children were screaming: Let them cross the border or they'll kill us! So what else could we do? Don't think I enjoy shooting at people. It's the first time this kind of thing has happened in all the time I've been here. Anyway, it wasn't my decision. First the general came down, then the prosecutor and some other guys from the district and the regional head-quarters. They were the ones who did the negotiating and made the promises. Then I get the order: don't let them through! Everything was decided somewhere else.' His classmate pointed toward the zenith, to where people have believed from time immemorial that the power deciding our fates resides.

Pavel turned off the main road, drove through a small wood and a sleeping village, then turned again on to a narrow road lined on both sides with ancient apple trees. A few minutes later he pulled up in front of the cottage. It stood alone, forlorn and dark. The meadow surrounding it was bathed in moonlight.

When he stepped inside he inhaled the familiar mixture of musty air, wood smoke and dried herbs. He turned on the light, opened the shutters, let down the flap of the writing-desk, poured himself a glass of vodka, turned on the television that stood on a small baroque table, sat down in an armchair and watched music videos for a while. He watched them to satisfy himself that videos, or at least those made according to the latest trends, were designed simply to bombard the viewer with disjointed bits of information and bizarre and deformed shapes until he finally comes to believe that the world is indeed an incomprehensible, perverted madhouse.

Recently, whenever he visited his mother and turned on her television, she would watch it for a while and then say: I've already seen that. It didn't matter what was on—the première of a film, the news or a sporting event: she'd already seen it. Yet she was almost wise in her dottiness. He turned the television off again. Two-thirty in the morning. He could go to bed now, but he still wouldn't sleep. He could sit down with his computer at the table and go on working on his screenplay, but he was too tired for that. He gazed for a while with pleasure at the intarsia on the cover of the writing-desk. The inlay formed the image of a man with a parrot sitting above his head. Not long ago his colleague and tennis partner, Sokol, had tried to sell him a commode with a similar motif, but he'd wanted too much for it.

How much was too much money? Nothing will ever be any cheaper. If he'd owned a real house and not just this isolated country cottage, which could be broken into and robbed at any time, he would have bought the commode. But he didn't have a house, and if he had, who would he bring to visit? His mother, perhaps. But his mother wouldn't know it was his house. She would only notice a change, and a change would be distressing. When he had been to see her the week before, he had found a photograph of his father. She had looked at him suspiciously. 'Who have you got there?'

'Don't tell me you don't know who it is.'

She hesitated for a moment, then said, 'Quite a handsome fellow your father was. You can take him away again now.'

So he'd taken the photo with him and put it in one of the drawers of the writing-desk. Now he got up and took it out. It was one of the first pictures he'd ever taken. It wasn't bad for a beginner. The contrast was very sharp, and his father's face looked as though it had been carved from wood, so in fact Pavel had succeeded in suggesting the man's profession.

His father had been a trained carpenter who did wood carving in his spare time. He had also liked to read biographies of famous people. His small library had introduced Pavel to Chaplin, Eisenstein, Hus, Balzac, Henry VIII, the unfortunate Maximilian Habsburg and the even less fortunate Anne Boleyn. Except for the last two, he had aspired to be somehow like each of them.

When he had had to move away from his father's house he abandoned reading and started going to the cinema. Unfortunately, the choice of films was limited, and most of them were very dull. They urged people to work harder and emulate the lives of revolutionaries, or they exposed the misery of the poor—in the present abroad and in the past at home. But he was moved by the story about Ditta's daughter. He saw it over and over again, as he did *The Ballad of a Soldier*. At the time he thought there could be nothing more magnificent than directing films, although that ambition seemed far beyond his reach. Eventually he grew tired of going to the cinema, but he didn't enjoy sitting at home either. He would wander through the woods on the edge of the city, sometimes with friends, more often with Lassie, his collie. The dog would hunt real or imaginary rabbits, while he would invent stories of which he himself was the hero, powerful and indomitable.

Then he decided to take pictures of things he saw on his rambles. He made the camera himself, partly because his mother couldn't afford a new one, and partly because he enjoyed making things and he wanted to have something unique. He used a cigar box, with the glass from an old pair of spectacles rigged as a lens. At first he took snapshots of everything he saw. When he showed his favourite ones to his mother, she gave them no more than a cursory glance: 'Well, so what? The camera did that, not you.'

He was stung and almost gave up altogether, but then he decided to prove to her that it was actually he who had made the pictures, and not the camera. He began to photograph clouds, animals and the hands of old people. To get pictures of hands, he went to an old people's home. He could have photographed their faces too, but he was more interested in hands. Everyone was doing faces. The worst films were full of them.

For animals, he went to the zoo. That was where he met Peter, and where they plotted their escape. He had actually had to persuade Peter to go through with it. Peter lacked the courage to do something like that on his own. He couldn't have brought himself to hurt his family. Parents, Peter believed, were to be honoured and obeyed. But Pavel had no family, only his mother, who believed that life had done her wrong and would do her more wrong; she constantly complained about her loneliness, her insomnia and her poor health.

Pavel poured himself another drink, lit a cigarette and opened a cupboard where he had stored carefully numbered cassettes.

He selected one, switched the television to the video mode, put a cassette in the VCR and sat down in the chair again.

A road, the border checkpoint, woods. A shot of a bus with children in it (a different bus with different children, of course), then the still photograph of a young man, the sole survivor. He hadn't been able to find pictures of the dead men. An officer in uniform appeared and pointed somewhere behind him. 'They came from that direction.'

'Did you have any warning?' his own voice said.

'Of course we did.'

'Did you have some kind of plan worked out?'

'It was hard to make a plan with those kids in the bus. Our priority was to get them out.'

'And if you hadn't been able to manage that?'

'We couldn't risk shooting as long as the children were in the bus.'

'So you'd have let them go across the border?'

'Only in the most extreme circumstances.'

'What does that mean?'

'The plan was to detain them as long as possible. To negotiate. That's what they've learned abroad—that as soon as hijackers agree to negotiate, you're halfway there. They won't start shooting. Certainly not at children.'

'Where did you stop them?'

'We stopped them twice.'

The officer pointed towards the checkpoint. 'Here's where we negotiated with them. When they let the kids go, we raised the barrier, but meanwhile a roadblock had been set up and sharpshooters were in place.'

The scene changed. The officer pointed to the places where the sharpshooters had been concealed. Then he pointed to a tree, its bark damaged by bullets, exposing the white wood beneath.

'And nothing happened to the other one?'

Off camera now, the officer replied, 'No. He'll go to the gallows without a scratch.' The voice laughed. 'I hope you're not recording this.'

He turned off the VCR and removed the cassette. The film was never broadcast.

Three-fifteen in the morning. He poured himself a final drink. His head was beginning to ache, and he felt an unpleasant constriction in his chest.

His bed was in the other room. Baroque carvings of saints stood on shelves, along with his father's carvings of non-saints. His father had liked carving birds most of all. Once he'd told Pavel that animals have one thing that puts them way ahead of people: they don't dissemble, and you don't have to pretend in front of them. He'd thought of that often in recent years. He was drawn to animals, and the films he made about them were usually better than his films about people.

He took off his shoes, his trousers and his shirt and crawled under the covers. Outside the window, tufts of white mist hung above the meadow. But the sky was clear and full of stars.

For a time, he put the nurse named Albina out of his mind. Then, unexpectedly, she cropped up again. He was lining up for a ski-lift and there she was, at the end of the queue. Her hair and part of her face were hidden under a red hood. Fortunately he could recall her face well.

'There, you see?' he said to her, 'I found you after all.'

They rode up the hill on the same bar, talking of nothing in particular. He could feel her hesitation, her wondering if she should accept this chance encounter as an omen. They skied downhill and waited for the lift together again. As they talked, he avoided any mention of his work, but since they were a short distance from the border, he told her about his abortive escape attempt so long ago. And he mentioned the prison term that followed. He contrived to surround his life with a mystery she might find attractive. At least she didn't try to prevent him from walking her to the door of her chalet.

The following evening they had dinner together. They continued to speak of nothing important. He sensed that her world was very different from his. There were forces at work in it in which he could not believe: faith in a higher law and an omnipresent power. She was prepared to look for evidence of this power in the position of the planets, and in omens. It occurred to him that she might bring a change for the better into his life.

3

ON SUNDAY AFTER lunch he went to visit his mother. He used to have lunch with her every Sunday, but in the past year she'd almost given up cooking and had her meals brought in. So he started coming after lunch; he couldn't bring himself not to come, leaving his mother all alone. Besides, her home was still his registered place of residence: he'd never tried to find somewhere else to move all his things. His bed was still there, and so was his desk, with its drawers stuffed with old letters and notebooks that no one would ever open. He'd carefully sorted the fading negatives of ancient photographs and stored them in two cupboards, and his old clothes, which no one would ever wear either, were gradually mouldering in the wardrobe in the hall.

Several weeks before, the last of his mother's friends had died, and now he was all she had left. She would sit inside all day, refusing to go out if he didn't go with her. She seemed increasingly gloomy and peculiar, full of dark suspicions about a world she understood less and less. He had not felt at ease in her presence for some time—if, indeed, he ever had. Still, he did remember moments of happiness in his childhood. His father enjoyed a joke, and his mother would laugh when he teased her. In the summer holidays she played tennis and volleyball with Pavel, and he liked listening to her talk about the theatre where she worked, though she was only a seamstress. It was a time when no decent play ever made it to the stage, and most of her work involved making Russian workers' blouses or miners' uniforms. She might have lived a completely different life had his father stayed with her. And so might Pavel.

'Is that you, Pavel?' Her surprise at his arrival was probably genuine; she was having trouble telling what day it was.

'I brought you something.' He took a pair of red slippers out of his bag and gave them to her. 'They have a fur lining.'

'Why do you waste your money?' She bent over with a suppleness that surprised him and slipped them on. 'They'll be wonderfully warm,' she said, straightening up again. She was a head shorter than he was, and small-boned. He'd inherited his father's height, but his build was more like hers.

'I'll make you tea,' she suggested.

'Thanks, but let's go out.'

'I bought some nice cakes.' She limped into the kitchen and he slipped into her room. He opened the linen cupboard and, from under a pile of towels, he took the tea caddy where she hid her money. He flipped open the lid and added two green banknotes to the box, closed it again and put it back.

His mother had never kept track of how much money she had. When he was growing up he used to take advantage of this and occasionally take some small change from her to buy a cinema ticket or cigarettes. She never knew, or if she did, she never let on. When he secretly gave her money now, he was merely repaying an old debt.

'Where are you, what are you up to?' she said from the other room.

Two steaming cups of tea were standing on the battered but clean table. His mother was just dusting sugar on the sweet buns. 'What are you doing these days?' she asked.

'I've just filmed a demonstration. And the day after tomorrow I'm going to the Castle. We're doing a documentary about the president.'

'Which one?'

'Ours. It's his birthday.'

'How old will he be?'

'Seventy-five.'

'He's younger than I am,' she said. 'I'm already old, aren't I?'

'There are people who are older,' he said.

'I can't stand to look at myself in the mirror any more.'

'I can't stand to look at myself either,' he said, and grimaced at the double meaning.

'I don't know, maybe you should be making films about more ordinary people,' she said. 'Someone like that could ruin you if he doesn't like what you do.'

'What if he does like it?'

'Then someone who doesn't like him could ruin you.'

'Why would anyone want to ruin me?'

'Because that's the way the world works, and you needn't talk so loud,' she said, lowering her voice and pointing to the wall. 'The whole world doesn't have to know. And your shirt's dirty. Why can't that woman of yours do a decent wash?'

'She does. And she's not my woman.'

'I don't understand that.'

'We're only sort of half together.'

'What does that mean, half together?'

'Come on, you know she's not my wife.'

'Well, it's still a disgrace,' said his mother. 'To have a man live with you and not marry him.'

'It's not her fault, it's mine. I don't want to get married.'

'Don't you love her enough?'

He shrugged his shoulders.

'It's time you settled down. Surely you don't want to be alone all your life? How much longer are you going to wait? Till I'm not here?'

'Oh, come on, Mother!' She didn't usually talk about her own death, but he was surprised that she still thought of herself as the only one who could relieve his loneliness. 'Why don't we go for a walk?'

She looked out of the window. 'I think I'd be cold. And I've hardly any feeling in my legs. I think we should just stay put. You're not rushing off, are you?'

'I'm playing tennis this evening.'

'Who with? Your father?'

'Oh, for heaven's sake, Mother! With Sokol, one of the producers. He's the one I went to Mexico with.'

'I don't know about any Mexico,' she said abruptly. 'Your father played tennis too.'

His father had died ten years ago. She hadn't gone to his funeral. He had left her, and in doing so had wronged her. Most people had wronged her, including Pavel. He had tried to flee the country when she needed him, aggravating the anxiety that plagued her. She could never see that it was his life and he had the right to live it according to his own lights. During the war, her father had been sent to a camp where he had perished. Her anxiety obviously had its beginnings in that experience, and she had seen nothing in her life since to persuade her it was groundless.

'He came to see me yesterday,' said his mother.

'Who?'

'Who were we talking about? Your father. He even brought me a ring to make it up to me. But I don't have it, so I probably didn't accept it. I can't remember.'

He should probably have tried to make her see the truth, but what good would that do? It was a harmless delusion, and perhaps it made her feel better.

'You shouldn't go anywhere else today. You look tired. You must be driving yourself too hard.' His mother cleared the teacups off the table and went to wash them.

'I'm going to call you "Sister",' he had suggested to Albina back then in the mountains.

'They all call me that at the hospital.'

'But it will mean something different to me.'

'What will it mean to you?'

'That I don't know anyone who is closer to me than you are.'

'How can you say that when you don't know me at all?'

'I'm serious. Besides, I like the word: Sister.'

'Stop it!'

'Do you like working there?'

'You mean in the hospital? I don't know. I don't know of anything better.'

'There are lots of other jobs. And you wouldn't have to watch people die.'

'Dying is part of life. And people who are dying need someone with them more than anyone else. Because . . . mostly they're not ready for it.'

'What do you mean?'

'When they're alive they don't think about death. And then when the moment comes they feel cheated. Death has caught up with them before they've had a chance really to live, before they've managed to understand what life is all about. They leave life before they've come to terms with death.'

'Have you come to terms with death?'

'I don't know,' she replied, 'but I try to live as fully as I can.'

'What does living fully mean?'

'It means not wasting time.'

'That's not a proper answer. What does not wasting time mean?'

'Being close to someone you love.'

'And what if you don't love someone?'

'Then you have to look for that person.'

It's odd that when they first talked of love they talked of death at the same time. Was this an omen? Or was it no more than a realization that love and death cannot be separated?

By summer they were living together. Once, they drove to a borrowed cottage. On the way he noticed a small clump of trees standing in a meadow, surrounded by crumbling walls. It was not hard to find an opening to squeeze through. When they had crawled through a tangled patch of bushes they came upon some old rain-worn stone slabs. Some were sticking at odd angles in the earth, others had been overturned and lay broken in the grass. They still bore traces of Hebrew lettering. He pulled his camera out of his bag and took a picture of a toppled gravestone.

'Why are you doing that?' she asked him.

'It's what I do.'

'You want to sell pictures of graves?'

'No. I only want to capture what's here.'

'The dead should be left in peace.'

'Am I disturbing them? I didn't knock these stones over.'

'Not everything needs to be captured.'

'Haven't you ever wanted to preserve the image of something that impressed you?'

'Not like that.'

'How then?'

'Inside me.'

Her remark made him angry. 'I'd soon die of starvation.'

What did it mean to preserve an image inside oneself?

To carry, for oneself, an intimation of what is hidden beneath the surface of a thing, of what you have liberated from it in the act of perceiving it.

Who might be interested in such images?

Someone who was also free.

What did it mean to be free?

'Pavel,' said his mother, 'why have you been silent for so long?'

'I'm glad just to be able to sit here beside you and not have to say anything.'

'And why are you sitting here with me? It can't be much fun.'

'You're my mother.'

'Yes,' she said, as though his answer surprised her. 'I am your mother.'

An hour later he walked on to the tennis-court in his whites. His adversary Sokol was almost ten years older than him and, although somewhat overweight, surprisingly agile. But agility couldn't save his game. He lacked the capacity for a good clean return, just as in his work he lacked precision in his use of language. But he made up for his verbal clumsiness with an acute political antenna; he was very sensitive to what went on beneath the apparently immobile surface of society. He could anticipate not only what was required at the moment, but also what would be required in the near future. Sokol's story ideas were always appropriate. He would have fits of dynamism, followed by periods of utter indifference to everything beyond his immediate surroundings. He liked to eat and drink well and when they were together in Mexico he preferred the beach or a shot of tequila *en la fonda* to work. Pavel could go along with him, or he could go off by himself and film whatever he wanted. It was a style of collaboration he liked because it placed no limits on him.

As usual he defeated his partner so quickly that he didn't even manage to tire himself out.

'I'm thinking,' Sokol said casually as they were showering, 'that it might make sense to start some kind of business. What would you say to setting up an advertising agency?'

'Me?'

'We'd be partners.'

'What would we make advertising for?'

'When private enterprise gets off the ground,' the producer explained, 'they'll need advertising. No ads, no business. Ads will be good biz, and TV ads will be the best biz of all.'

'Advertising isn't my speciality.'

'That's all propaganda is—just advertising.'

'You think what I do is propaganda?' he asked defensively.

The producer mumbled something into his towel. He didn't like to argue and he didn't like direct questions.

But Sokol was right, he thought. Their films were commercials for a way of life that no one would buy if it were for sale, including him. And it would be good business.

'It's never even crossed my mind,' he said. 'There's no private enterprise—how could there be any advertising?'

'Suppose things change?'

'If things change, the two of us won't be making any money out of it.'

'Why not? It will only depend on what you can do. And who is more skilled than you? That's all advertising is, ideas and skill.'

If it only depended on what he could do, he would try to apply his skill somewhere else in some other way. He would film his own screenplays. He knew they were better than the ones that were being made and given prizes.

They came out of the showers, had a glass of vodka and chatted for a while about how things might change. Sokol had a scenario of his own. He thought there would be a series of gradual changes that would begin as official policy but quickly gain an unstoppable momentum. The initiators of change would be swept aside, and the world in which they lived would collapse.

Pavel listened carefully, wondering what kind of role his colleague imagined for himself after the collapse. He remembered that long ago, he too had been obsessed with ideas of change. He had even dreamed of it. In prison, his dreams became so intense that he almost believed it would happen. But now he could no longer imagine it and preferred not to think about it.

When they parted Sokol said, 'Don't forget, next week we're filming in the Castle.'

Apparently he did not expect the changes to happen in the immediate future. Otherwise he would surely have found a way to send someone else to the Castle in his place.

4

THE FILMING WAS over. Pavel wasn't sure if they had anything they could use. They had had to work magic with the lights to hide the fact that the old man could no longer move his left arm and to soften the ingrained harshness in his face. And Pavel's job was the easier. Sokol, who was conducting the interview, had the worst of it. It was no small task to coax lively and interesting remarks, let alone original ideas, out of the head of state. For years he'd been repeating the same thing over and over again: vague hopes that people, ignoring their own experience, would accept the aims and values he still espoused. At one point he appeared to be on the verge of saying something heartfelt. 'In religious instruction they used to teach us that if we believed, our faith would save us. We changed that old-fashioned doctrine: believe only what stands the test of reason. But . . . ' He stopped, then waved his hand dismissively. It must have been frustrating for Sokol. Half a thought was useless. A president dismissing his own idea with a wave of his hand was something they would never allow him to show on television.

If only the man who had been the president for so many years could do something genuinely appealing, something they could capture on film—ride a horse, play tennis, levitate. It was said he had been a sheet-metal worker when he was in prison. No one, of course, had filmed him doing it, and today they preferred to remain silent about that period of his life. There were miles of old tapes in the archives, but they were all the same: a gloomy old man standing behind a microphone, making a speech, shaking hands with one group of statesmen, kissing another, inspecting a guard of honour, boarding or getting off an aeroplane, embracing the comrades—now seeing him off, now submissively awaiting his return. There were also shots of the leader waving to cheering crowds, accepting ceremonial offerings from villagers in folk costumes, and bouquets from terrified little girls. In some he still looked young, full of energy and authority. But it all amounted to desperate and uniform tedium.

What was tedium?

Time filled with encounters that leave no mark on us.

If only the president had some special objects around him that were really his, like a terrarium with snakes, or a stuffed bear, or a parrot in a cage. Or if he'd had some dynamic and interesting people in his entourage. But the only people he could bear to have near him were an ancient maid, who had been with him since his youth and survived both his wives, and two valets. And somewhere in the background, you could still sense the presence of a whole cabal with whom he had once conspired to gain

control, and from whom he could never completely disso-
ciate himself, bound as he was to them by common actions
and crimes.

The lighting technicians rolled up their cables and
carried away their lamps and reflectors. Once more, the
room became a pristine and aristocratic antechamber.
Though Pavel would not have admitted it, it made him feel
good to be here, able to move about freely in this setting.
The double doors leading into a series of adjoining
chambers remained open, and he observed that enormous
crystal chandeliers were prodigally ablaze throughout the
entire wing of the castle.

The old man stood up, walked over to them and shook
hands, first with Sokol and then with him. 'Thank you. For
your efforts,' he said, attempting a smile. He was clearly
wondering whether to go on. 'Would you like to stay for a
drink?' he said finally.

The invitation was a surprise and clearly impossible to
refuse. The old man motioned to them and they followed
him into an adjoining room where an obliging waiter was
standing with a tray of glasses ready to offer them. The
president sat down in an armchair, which meant that they
too could sit down, and even speak to him. The old man
who now sat opposite them had the power to grant any of
their wishes, though why should he use his power for that?

'To your health, comrades!' said the president, raising
his glass.

And what did Pavel wish for? To gain a top position in
his profession? It was hardly the best time for that. To film
his own screenplay? It wasn't the right time for that either.
This particular leader would hardly understand his screen-
plays. Should he mention that his superiors had recently
banned his innocuous documentary on life in a psychiatric
hospital? The president had more important things to worry
about than a film about the mentally ill. The most he could
do would be to appoint someone to investigate; Pavel's
bosses would be interrogated and eventually the whole
thing would be turned against him.

'So, what do you think of the present situation?' asked
the old man, peering at them through his thick glasses. His

question caught them off guard. What did he want to hear? The truth? Or another one of the comforting cock-and-bull stories he must hear every day?

'What do people think in your line of work, in television?' Fortunately, he either didn't expect an answer or he immediately forgot that he had asked a question. The president reminded him of his mother, except that his mother was not in power, and she had no maid and no valets to wait on her hand and foot.

'The situation isn't exactly ideal,' the old man went on. 'Unfortunately, it would appear that we haven't been able to maintain the standards that our people have come to expect. You know, a man may be on top, but he can still be helpless. I do everything in my power. Sixteen hours a day. I would need three lives, not all of this.' He waved a finger in the air, as if to rebuke the luxury around them. 'To serve a good cause and change the world, that is what we must do. But who still wants that? And who can carry it off? When we were young, we had a different kind of enthusiasm. We were ready to suffer, even to go hungry, but we knew we were fighting for a cause, for an order that was more just. Sometimes we didn't have enough for supper, but I managed to save enough for the train that took me to meet the comrades who were waiting for me that evening.'

'Was that when you were in university?' asked Sokol.

'In university, before university and after university. Sometimes it was better and sometimes it was worse, but it was never easy. When we were children'—the old man's eyes now had a distant look—'we used to go barefoot most of the year, except in winter. On mornings when the dew fell, it was bitterly cold. But no one wants to hear about that any more. When I finally got a pair of shoes, they were hand-me-downs from my sisters,' he went on, giving in to the flow of memories, 'but I could only wear them on Sundays for church.' He stopped, as though he were suddenly afraid he had said too much.

At last the old man was talking about himself, but, unfortunately, not on camera. Had he spoken about his childhood for the record, Pavel could then have added footage of his native village, dug up some snapshots of his parents who were only simple labourers—that is if the president hadn't falsified his biography to fit the legend of a leader who had emerged from the bosom of the people to serve the people. His mother had died when he was a baby, and by his own account he had not had an easy childhood.

'All the same, those years were better than what came afterwards. The comrades were still true to the very core and wouldn't betray each other even under torture. And my first wife was still alive.' His voice had taken on a tone of regret, and he quickly reached for a glass to conceal the fact. 'But then everything changed. I found myself in the clutches of the executioner, and he was working round the clock. The worst of it was that our own people turned me in, turned the best of us over to him. At least, they pretended to be our people. They were all protestations of loyalty, but their knives were out. I wrote letters proving my innocence. They didn't reply. I demanded that they at least produce witnesses, but they never materialized. The executioners came up with a punishment for me: six years in solitary confinement with no news of the world, no visits from my family. Six years when the only faces I saw were their faces, executioners' faces. And where do you think these people are now?' He took another drink. 'They say they are restructuring things for the better,' he said, suddenly animated, 'but all they will accomplish is to tear down what is still hanging together—not entirely, but somewhat. And when they've torn it down they'll try to shift the blame on to me. That's how it has always been done. But a time will come when they will say, "The good was buried with his bones."' He laughed drily, then added, 'The torture we withstood! Money will destroy us. They are selling out everything to get it: ideas and each other.'

When people said 'they,' they usually meant those in power. Who did the head of state include in this little word? Those who were under him. Those who surrounded him. Everyone else.

Again the waiter appeared with his tray. The president shook his head, the waiter held the tray out to them, but they too refused, not daring to take another glass when their host was no longer drinking.

'Don't forget to send me the film as soon as it's ready,' the president said. 'Not that I want to censor you, but you know how it is. At my age I might not live long enough to see it.'

'I'll do that,' Sokol promised.

The president stood up. The informal audience was over. Pavel hadn't used it to any advantage. Perhaps it could not have been used to any advantage anyway, because life and power only appeared to reside in such places. Where did they really reside?

He wasn't certain of the answer. And the thought disturbed him.

FILM

I

A WEDDING PARTY streams out of the main entrance of the town hall. A tall man with a camera steps out in front of them. He has to crouch slightly to get them all in his viewfinder. That is if he wants to get the rest of the square in the picture as well. Further down, a demonstration is brewing.

The sun is peeking out from behind a tower. The wedding guests squint while trying to put on appropriately happy expressions.

'Please don't stop because of me.'

The groom is small, elderly and plump; the bride is half a head taller, at least fifteen years younger, has long, fair, almost white hair, like the photographer's. They could even be related, but for him this is probably just another job, or perhaps an excuse to get a camera into the area inconspicuously.

'Now I'd like the bride in the centre, the groom on her left.' He squeezes the shutter and then changes his lens.

The newly-weds disappear from the viewfinder, and the photographer now watches the demonstrators, the uniformed police officers and the militia.

'Thank you. Now if the others would just step to one side slightly, and the groom just a touch to the right. That's right, thank you,' and he presses the shutter. Then he bows slightly, shakes hands with the wedding guests and walks away. As soon as he turns the corner, two men block his way. The older man looks like a shabby office clerk; the second, who has long hair and is wearing jeans, reminds him of a drummer in an underground band.

The older man shows him some ID. 'Well, Mr Fuka! What are we taking pictures of today?'

The photographer is taken aback. He'd like to hide his camera, but he can't. 'A wedding.'

The man who showed him the ID points to the camera. 'I thought you'd given up photography.'

The photographer holds the camera behind his back, perhaps in a childlike belief that if it can't be seen it doesn't exist. 'I'm working the night shift now.'

'We'll check your story. Whose wedding was it?'

'An acquaintance of mine.'

'Can you tell us his name?'

'No. I don't see why I should.'

'We'll find out anyway. Are you willing to hand over your film voluntarily?'

'No, why should I?'

'Maybe to save yourself a trip.' Both men wait for his reply.

The photographer looks around to see if there is any hope of escape, but the square is teeming with men in uniform, so he shrugs his shoulders and asks, 'Does that mean I'm under arrest?'

The younger man speaks for the first time. 'Why under arrest already? Do you feel guilty or something?'

'Unfortunately,' he replies, 'whether I feel guilty or not has nothing to do with it. Neither do actions.'

'In other words, you'd rather come with us?'

The photographer shrugs his shoulders. He probably can't save his film, but he won't surrender it voluntarily. They have no right to demand it from him.

They lead him away to an ugly, poorly lit room in a nondescript tenement house where they fire questions at him which, for the most part, he does not answer. They want to know about a friend of his who is working as a caretaker in a castle, and about the friend's wife. They even ask about the woman with whom he's now living, but to whom he is not yet married.

'If you'd behave a little more reasonably,' says the older man, 'you could do better than working as a stoker in a hotel boiler-room. After all, you graduated from the film academy. You've even made a few documentaries about animals. Or have I got that wrong?'

'What does behaving reasonably mean?'

'You must see enough reasonable people around you to give you the right idea,' says the rock drummer.

'You certainly shouldn't be taking pictures of an act of protest organized by the enemies of the state,' the older man advises. 'Maybe you've been promised a bundle for those pictures by some foreign agencies, but I assure you, when you work out your profits and your losses, you'll come up very much on the short side.'

He replies that no one has offered him money for anything, that he's not selling his pictures to agencies or private individuals. He is only taking them for his own pleasure.

The last thing they do is give him a piece of paper stating that they've confiscated the film from his camera. Then they let him go.

That evening he complains to the woman he's living with about losing his film. Unfortunately, he had shots of the demonstration on it, along with the wedding pictures. He thinks he's in real trouble.

'You should have been more careful,' says his girlfriend. The second piece of good advice he's been given today.

'I'm being as careful as I possibly can,' he says testily.

'Maybe you should do something about it.'

'What do you mean?'

'There's a woman, one of my customers,' she says. 'Her husband works in the film archives. He chooses films for the government types and bigwigs to watch. And he picks films for the Castle.'

'Why are you telling me this?'

'Apparently he likes films about animals, and especially about snakes,' she says, stressing the word 'he', to leave him in no doubt that she means the man whose primary residence is the Castle. 'If they sent him one of your films, maybe he'd go for it.'

'I don't give a damn if he'd go for it or not.'

'But he might be able to help you.'

'Don't you think he has other things on his mind?'

'Well, maybe not him. The fellow from the archives must know lots of influential people. He might be able to arrange something.'

'Stop right there. I don't want to hear any more.'

'I only thought . . . ' She falls silent. He gets up from the table and goes into the other room. For a while he paces up and down like an animal in a cage. Then he stops at the window. He looks out at the metal fence. Cars are parked behind it, among piles of scrap metal. The fence reminds him of the fence on the border. He turns away and thinks of a woman he once loved, the only woman he was ever really fond of. He sees her in a white nurse's uniform walking down the long hospital corridor. He calls her by a name that has a foreign sound to it. He calls, he almost pleads: Ali, Alina. But the woman walks on, not hearing him, or at least pretending not to hear him.

II

A NARROW GRID of sunlight falls into the cell. When the gavel came down and they gave him the rope, they shoved him into a better cell. Now, when Robert stands on his toes, he can even see some hilltops out there. But they've stuck this Gabo character in with him—a halfwit pervert who molests and then murders little girls and howls with terror when he thinks of what's coming, and on top of that his stupid face reminds him of that idiot Míla who got him into this mess in the first place and then goes and dies, leaving him to take the rap. When they give a guy the rope, they leave him alone. So he doesn't have to beat metal or polish glass beads . . . but it also means he's got nothing to help him drive out the boredom, drive out the thoughts that plague him.

Like Gabo, he was issued with one book, several magazines and a chess set. They can forget the chess set because neither of them knows how to play. Gabo's old cellmate had tried to explain the rudiments of the game, but nothing can penetrate that thick skull. Gabo can't read either, so once he's made his bed and washed himself, there's nothing left to do. From morning wake-up to lights out Gabo paces up and down the cell. The only time he stops is to swallow a couple of mouthfuls of grub or straighten his slippers or gape at his own enormous freckled paws, the ones he used to strangle those pathetic little girls. Sometimes he mumbles a few words about how he did it, but without regret, absent-mindedly, as though he was talking about somebody else, or about something completely unimportant. More often, he starts wailing in a high voice like a dog howling, or like a siren blowing.

It's enough to drive you crazy, but the strange thing is Robert gets used to it after a while and stops paying attention. He tries to read. Fortunately, one book can last him a whole week. What the inmates' library has on offer is strictly anodyne. The librarian usually sends historical novels, so for the first time in his life he is learning about something that has nothing to do with his life. Savage landscapes, ancient codes of honour, banquets, tournaments, torture chambers, executions, romantic love, strange foreign names like Robespierre, Gandhi and Anne Boleyn. What fascinates him about Anne Boleyn's story is that if the king wanted to get rid of an inconvenient wife, he didn't have to strangle her, he just had her head cut off. He tries to convey this new insight to Gabo, but Gabo doesn't see what he's getting at. If only he didn't remind him of Míla and of everything that happened, everything they so hopelessly screwed up. He tries to persuade Gabo to listen to the whole story over and over again, because even that idiot should be able to understand that their plan was flawless and it was Míla who ruined everything. They keep an eye out for a bus full of brats. No one will dare shoot at that. They easily get aboard with their hunting rifles, and he shouts a line at the driver that he's been dying to use ever since he was last in prison, when the thought of it

49

kept him going. 'Put your fucking foot down! We're going to the border.'

Little girls start screaming behind him, but he doesn't even bother to turn around. He just watches where they're going. They're at the barricades in half an hour, and when they open the little window they unload a few rounds into the guardhouse so the sentries will know they're serious. They get the message fast and start running about, scared shitless, begging for Robert and Míla to be patient till the brass come.

Then some general in civvies shows up and starts trying to butter them up. They should have blown him away, wiped their arses with him, but Míla—damn that son of a bitch—starts talking to him. Either he's lost it or it makes him feel good to have this general cringing in front of him, a miserable private, promising the fucking sky if he'll just let the kids go. And then more brass show up and they all swear on their honour—their honour, for Christ's sake!—that they'll let them cross the line, and they'll even let them have the driver—one hostage ought to be enough, right?—and Míla really does lose it. Well, they both do when they believe them, those double-crossing bastards who'd never spoken the truth in their lives, not even by accident. And he let it happen. He forgot that when he broke his leg, when they stabbed him with a knife in a fight, when they didn't let him eat for two days in the kids' home where he'd been left to rot, no one ever lifted a fucking finger for him, no one thought of him as a human being—and he was no older and no worse than these brats on the bus. But it actually makes him feel good when they talk to him, make promises, call him 'Sir'. So they go along with it and let the kids out of the bus. Then the barrier swings up, and they cheer, but those double-dealing swine block the road further on with an armoured car and, before they know they've been had, flames start spewing at them from all sides.

It's something he's only seen in films, but a steady stream of flame actually pours from the gun barrels. He catches only a glimpse of it before he hits the floor, and Míla's body falls down beside him, Míla screaming like a madman, and more in surprise than terror he sees a row of holes popping across the windscreen, the cracks in the glass zigzagging in all directions, and he watches the glass collapse and sees the driver's body go rigid behind the steering-wheel and then slide down beside Míla, drenched in blood. The full horror hits him and without a thought he edges to the door, rolls down the steps, right up against the door, and later he realized that was what saved him because those motherfuckers were raking the bus high, shooting into the windows and through the seats. So he curls up against the closed door, shouting, 'You mother-fuckers, you motherfuckers,' though he can't hear his own voice over the din.

At last there's silence, but he doesn't dare move or look around or even examine himself. He hears footsteps, one of those motherfuckers yanks the door open and he's looking into the barrel of a machine-gun, and someone yells, 'Hands up!', like they do in films, but instead he just rolls out of the bus on to the ground, straight into a puddle of petrol leaking out of the bullet-ridden tank.

Míla is already dead; the driver is still groaning. They put cuffs on him and take him to the customs shed.

He's been inside twice, always the kind of slammer where you could work out ways to survive. Now they toss him into a hole all by himself, and they only take him out for interrogations. They try to get him to confess that someone has put him up to this and told him what to do, that he's a terrorist and a murderer who shot the poor driver, a father of two. Mostly he keeps his mouth shut because how could these bastards understand anyway? He'd only wanted to clear out of this god-forsaken shithole country where the one thing they care about is having him work his arse off and then give a public display of how happy that makes him. Then he gets the rope.

Robert doesn't know what else there is to say. If he could talk to this moron, maybe the two of them could find a way of making a run for it, even though he can't imagine how they'd break out of this hole, let alone from death row, then get over a five-metre wall and slip past the machine-gun nests at each corner of the outer perimeter. But at least they'd be making some kind of mental effort, rather than just waiting for the door to open and the guard to call their names and say, get your things, or on second thoughts, don't bother, you won't be needing them any more.

There's a rattling in the lock, and then the bolt slides back and the door opens. He stiffens. He's always terrified when the guard appears unexpectedly. He stands to attention, looks into the guard's expressionless eyes and gives the regulation response. No, this can't yet be it. He's put in a request for clemency, and they can't have turned it down so quickly—if they had, they'd have had to let him know.

The guard handcuffs him and lets him walk out of the cell. Two more guards are waiting in the corridor and they motion him to go with them. This is the only moment when he might try making a run for it: with cuffs on his hands, two escorts on his heels, in a locked corridor. Right.

Now he's only got the strength to think about where they're taking him and why. Maybe they have turned down his appeal and taken pity on Gabo because they think trying to get out of the country is a worse crime than strangling little girls. Now they're taking him to the yard, or wherever it is they put up their fucking gallows.

They enter the lift and go down to the ground floor. His lawyer is waiting for him in the visitors' room. He's been assigned to Robert's case, he's a state-appointed lawyer, a young man with a ruddy complexion and a high forehead. When he speaks, the veins on it stand out. Robert, of course, doesn't know whether he's a good lawyer or a swine like all the rest of them. Probably the latter, although he'd been taken aback when the lawyer tried to persuade that rat in robes that he, Robert, had had no intention of killing anyone, as proved by the fact that he allowed all the children off the bus.

The lawyer, a tall, thin man, rises slowly and quietly to greet him. 'There are just a few small items, Mr Bartoš,' he says, and in this place, the formal salutation almost sounds like an insult: 'We've submitted the request and we can expect an answer within four weeks.'

'What kind of answer?'

'We have to hope for the best. But I've got two pieces of good news for you.'

Robert looks at him expectantly.

'When I asked you last time about the exact date of your birth it was because I have an acquaintance who is involved in astrology and wanted to do your horoscope.'

'I don't know—I don't understand what you're talking about.'

'You don't know what a horoscope is?'

He shakes his head.

'It's an attempt to predict someone's future from the position of the planets at the moment of his birth,' explains the lawyer. 'Unfortunately, we don't know the exact hour of your birth,' he adds regretfully.

'My mum never told me. They locked her up when I was little and that finished her off. She only came back to die.'

'I know,' says the lawyer quickly, 'but my friend managed to chart your approximate horoscope, and he found that very event in it. All of last year was a very critical time for you, especially May and September. But this year you have several promising conjunctions.' The lawyer suddenly leans towards him and says, almost in a whisper, 'We've managed to establish a contact with the man who will decide on your appeal for clemency. This is very important. You know how these things work.'

'Thanks,' he says. The lawyer never speaks directly. It's difficult to understand what he's actually talking about.

'We have to hope for the best. We've done everything in our power. Everything else is in God's hands. Do you believe that, Mr Bartoš?'

'I don't know.' The lawyer is acting strangely today. He seems too formal and too ingratiating. It scares him.

'You ought to believe. It would certainly make your wait easier.'

'I don't really know much about it,' he replies, trying to be polite.

'Yes, well, I didn't think so. Anyway, that's all I really wanted to say. Any complaints about your treatment?'

He shakes his head.

'Good,' nods the lawyer. 'So we have to believe—*you* have to believe—in that horoscope.' The lawyer lowers his voice again. 'And in our contact with the man who can give you clemency.' Then, in a normal tone, he says, 'I'm quite optimistic about your case. Try to think about the mercy of God, even though you don't know much about it. People in your situation sometimes discover these things for themselves. There must be someone standing above all this. Above the world, above justice, above history—you know what I'm saying?'

Robert says nothing. He stares at the table in front of him. Someone has carved graphic representations of the female pudenda in it, along with some kind of caption. The words have been scratched out, but the symbols remain.

The lawyer leans close to him and asks in a whisper, 'Now that it's all over, I mean now that we've submitted our appeal, I wanted to ask you, Mr Bartoš, why did you do it? What could you possibly have been thinking?'

So the guy was probably just one of them after all, who had been given the job of dragging a last-minute confession out of him. 'Like I told you already, we wanted out.'

'Yes,' nods the lawyer, 'you did say that. But why? What were you expecting on the other side? Did you think you wouldn't have to work there either?'

'The hell I thought that!' His face flushes in a sudden rush of anger. 'Why don't you just bugger off, you stupid prick!'

III

THE CONVOY CONSISTS of two yellow-and-white police cars, three ugly, heavily chromed black limousines with white blinds covering the side windows, then one final police car.

The ornamental wrought-iron gates swing open, the vehicles drive through the gateway, past a cluster of box trees and rose-beds, and pull up in front of the entrance to the château. A valet is waiting at the bottom step. He bows, steps up to one of the limousines and opens the door, then utters the official salutation: 'Honour to work, and good evening, Comrade President.'

An old man is sitting in the car, alone. At one time his body must have been tall and sturdy. Now it is bent with age. His dark eyes are almost lost under bushy eyebrows, and he looks blankly through a pair of thick glasses at the man holding the door open. Then his eyes flash in sudden recognition. The old man turns, reaches for a briefcase lying on the seat beside him and hands it to the valet. Then he swings his legs out of the car and plants them heavily on the ground. 'Yes, that's right,' he says, and with his eyes fixed unseeingly ahead of him, he climbs the stairs and goes through the main entrance into the hall. Then he stops and hesitates. 'What time is it?'

'It's just eight, Comrade President.'

'I can't possibly sleep before midnight. What are we going to do?'

'Shall I call the projectionist?'

The old man shakes his head almost imperceptibly.

'The librarian? Or your maid?'

The old man hesitates a moment, then shakes his head, walks through the hall and enters the conservatory where he keeps snakes in terraria. He stops in front of the terrarium where the Gabon viper lives. He leans close to the glass and appears to be examining the horn coming out of the centre of the serpent's flat skull. 'My poor dear wife liked them,' he says. Tears run down his cheeks. With his back still to the valet, he gives an order. 'Tea in my study.'

Two of the four walls of his study are covered, floor to ceiling, with shelves full of books, but he hasn't had time to read them for years. Now he walks past the bookshelves and stops at a table on which a neatly stacked pile of folders stands between two telephones. He opens the top folder and leafs through it, looking around the room as he does so. He closes the folder again, walks over to the window, leans on the sill and, hidden by the curtains, looks out into the garden. Pathways sifted with bright white sand diverge, converge and criss-cross over well-kept lawns, and on the upper part of a slope, windblown bushes and purple rhododendrons have scattered their petals on the grass. In the lower section, among the boulders of a rock garden, three men potter about, pretending to plant something.

Perhaps they are real gardeners, but he never knows what the people around him are—what they *really* are.

For a moment he considers going into the garden and speaking to one of them, asking him what his real job here is, or what he really thinks. What do you think about our new society? What do you expect from the future?

Genuine gardeners or not, they would still not answer him truthfully. They've been chosen carefully and trained even more carefully. Not about flowers, but about what to say if they should meet him.

One of the men is now coming down the path with a bouquet of white flowers in his hand, walking towards the château. The president watches him until the man disappears into the entrance, then he turns, walks away from the window and sits down in a deep armchair. He reaches out for the folder he was looking at earlier, leafs through it again and examines at the clusters of letters whose individual shapes he can no longer distinguish.

Someone knocks on the door, and when he gives permission to enter, the valet comes in with the soundless tread of a cat. He is bringing flowers and tea. With fluid movements he sets the china cups and saucers on the glass table-top, then puts the vase with the white flowers on the window-ledge. The valet is a small, thin man. His greyish-yellow face is indecipherable. It reveals neither willingness not deference.

'What's that you've brought?'

'Your favourite white peonies, Comrade President.'

'My favourite?' whispers the president. 'It was my wife who loved them, my poor wife. She loved to look at them. I . . . ' He stops. Then he adds: 'Just recently, I find things are blurred. They want me to have an operation'—he points to his eyes—'but I'll be hospitalized, and what will happen here? Then the doctors with the knives—who will assure me that they are genuine doctors?' He stops, because he has said something that he could have said to his wife, with whom   he   still   carries   on   conversations, although not usually in front of the valet. He reaches for the cup of tea and dismisses the valet with a wave of his hand.

Indeed, since his wife's tragic death, he speaks to her more often than he did when she was alive. Perhaps it's because now she can be near him at all times.

After the valet has left, he complains to her that his comrades are increasingly plotting against him and spreading malicious gossip among the people through the familiar channels.

His wife, God rest her soul, thinks he should do something to regain the people's favour. He could lower prices, or grant someone a special favour.

Favour for whom? he wonders.

Has he already forgotten that when he came to power, years ago, he had had to banish from public life many important officials who refused to acknowledge the immutable reality of his government? That he got rid of most of the old guard and disbanded most of the military command units? That he drove professors from the universities and silenced all the journalists, film-makers and writers who had displayed the slightest sign of insubordination? Some of the more defiant ones escaped abroad, and several ended up in prison. But most of them had taken refuge in the twilight zone of menial work in warehouses, boiler-rooms and other places of asylum. What if he were to show magnanimity towards some of them? Doing so would certainly spark hope in many others, thus dulling their resistance to his government and throwing his enemies into disarray. He could even grant clemency to someone condemned to death, and so enhance his reputation abroad. He recalls how he himself had once waited in a cell for a trial in which it seemed the only possible outcome was the death sentence, though he was completely innocent. They condemned him to life in prison.

At the time, oddly enough, he hadn't worried about death, nor thought about the hopelessness of his situation. On the contrary, he imagined himself coming out of prison and returning to the comrades from whom he had been forcibly separated by his enemies' intrigues, and he was certain that he would continue towards his ultimate goal of being first among them all. He imagined that once he finally held the reins of government in his hands, he would summon everyone who had wronged him: the interrogators who had tortured him for long days and nights to drag absurd confessions out of him, and the prison guards who had tormented him with thirst and cold, or had dragged him into freezing, damp solitary confinement for the slightest misdemeanour. And of course he would summon the public prosecutor, a successful and dedicated son of the nation and the working people, who had railed against him as though he were a sell-out and a traitor; and the false witnesses; and the scheming chairman of the tribunal who didn't hesitate to condemn him for the duration of his life to prison. He would have them all summoned and lined up in the hall where he usually received foreign dignitaries and heads of state and he would ask them to say what they thought of him now? And he'd watch them sweat with terror, and he would be amused as they fumbled to explain that they had always admired him, that they had merely obeyed orders and had acted against their own convictions.

He had only made the first and most difficult of his dreams come true: he had become the head of state, the first man in the country. Yet those who had once stood in judgement over him went on judging, and his interrogators went on interrogating. He preferred not to look into what had become of them. He now understood that all those who had wronged him were virtually indistinguishable from those who had not. The latter had simply never been given the opportunity. The difference was only that fear had now transformed those who had genuinely wronged him into loyal supporters.

His wife, God rest her soul, is now waiting for an answer. Yes. He will do something, but when the right time comes. Tomorrow a nigger from some country—and he doesn't even know where it is—is arriving on an official visit. He still has to read his briefing papers and check the menu to make sure they haven't forgotten to include the fillet of trout meunière.

Yes, he will make a grand gesture, but it won't accomplish anything. Everyone is just waiting for him to trip up so they can push him out. That's the way people are: envious, only out for themselves. Given half a chance, they would raze their houses to the ground, reduce bridges to nuts and bolts, roads to cobblestones, machines to gearwheels; they would grind bones into dust. They would burn everything down, for fire is their passion. From his study of history, he knows that people are arsonists at heart. They look at churches, castles and palaces and dream of seeing them go up in flames.

And against all of these forces, he now stands alone. All he has left are chauffeurs, gardeners, valets and doctors, and he cannot be certain that they really are chauffeurs, gardeners, valets and doctors.

The old man weeps. Then he makes a decision and presses a button. The valet enters almost at once, as though he had been poised in readiness just outside the door.

'I'd like a drink,' he commands. 'Do we have a drop of that good cognac left?'

'Of course, Comrade President.'

'Bring me two glasses, comrade,' he orders and then watches the valet open the door of a small refrigerator concealed among the bookshelves and remove an onion-shaped bottle containing golden-brown liquid. The two enormous glasses have stems of unequal length. He will receive the taller one. The valet pours the liquid into both glasses and waits.

'Sit down,' he commands.

'Thank you, Comrade President.' The valet sits stiffly on a leather seat, ready to leap to his feet again at any moment.

'What's your name again?'

'Karel Houska, Comrade President.'

The president nods. The name sounds familiar, and no doubt he's asked about it before. 'Well, drink up then.'

The valet grasps his glass and says ceremoniously: 'If you will allow me, Comrade President, to toast your health.'

The valet takes a sip, but the president downs the entire glass in a single gulp. He knows it is inappropriate to drink this way and doesn't do so when taking part in official toasts, but here there is no need to stand on ceremony. 'Powerful stuff, eh!'

'Powerful, Comrade President.' The valet refills his glass.

'Pour yourself some too,' the president orders, and then asks, 'Are you married?'

'I am, Comrade President.'

'Doesn't she mind it when you're on duty like this?'

'She's used to it by now.'

'And what did you do before? Were you in service then too?'

'I was a waiter. It was less responsible, but the work was harder.'

'You're happy here, I take it?'

'I'm very honoured, Comrade President, to have this position.'

'And what do people say?' he asks, thinking he may learn something. 'Do they ask you a lot of questions?'

'Perhaps they would, but no one knows I work here.'

'What about your wife?'

'If you tell anything to a woman, Comrade President, it's like putting it in the papers.' The valet's face remains expressionless.

'Go on, drink!' he urges.

The valet ceremoniously raises the glass, holds it for a moment at eye-level and then takes a sip.

'Do you have any children?'

'Yes, I do, Comrade President. Two.'

'Are they at school?'

'They've finished school, Comrade President. One's a soldier, the other's an engineer.'

'Very good,' he praises him. 'We need soldiers and we need engineers. Do they have good positions?'

'They can't complain.'

The old man nods. This valet seems like quite a nice fellow. He knows that one of his valets is a nice, sincere, steady fellow, and perhaps this is the one. The other one probably has two children too. Everyone seems to have two children, or at least they claim to. 'Do you have their pictures with you?'

'As a matter of fact, I do, Comrade President.'

He takes a wallet from the breast pocket of his perfectly tailored jacket and removes two pictures.

The president looks blankly at the unfamiliar faces. 'Fine-looking lads,' he says. 'You can be proud of them.'

He hears a faint creaking behind him and turns his head slightly as if to reassure himself that all the books are in place.

They are, of course. But there, in front of the bookshelf, the ends of its legs buried in the thick nap of the carpet, is that thing again, standing there as it does almost every evening: a bier holding an open coffin. Tonight there's only one, but some evenings there are so many, packed so closely together, that you can scarcely get by them. Today they only managed to get one of them in. His wife is lying in the coffin. He can almost see her features under the immaculate white sheet. They never want him to raise the sheet. They say the sight of her would be too awful. Her body was damaged beyond recognition in the fall, they say. He always obeys them, though their only aim is to torment him and gradually hound him to death. This is why they push her in here every evening, and all those others too, most of whom he doesn't know and for whose death he bears no guilt. Like those nine miners they brought in last Sunday. Some of them hadn't even had their disfigured faces properly covered. Was he to blame for their deaths? Was it he who ordered the Sunday shifts? And even if he had, wasn't everyone complaining that they weren't getting enough coal? There was always something unavailable, something forgotten, something neglected, and then people died, poisoned by bad water, smothered by toxic exhalations, blown to smithereens, exposed to radiation—although experts assured him that no one had been exposed to radiation—killed by impurities in the medicine, or by the lack of any medicine at all. And then they parade the bodies in here to haunt him. Once, he'd slipped out of a reception for some generals to find that they had filled the whole corridor with stretchers and, because there were so many, had stacked them along the walls four deep, like bunk-beds. It was hideous and it was disgraceful. And he had no choice but to squeeze past them and pretend not to see anything.

The valet refilled the president's glass.

'Take some yourself, lad.' He should ask the valet to

have her taken away, but God knows who the valet really is. Maybe he's with them. 'What did you do before you came here?'

'I was a waiter, Comrade President,' replies the valet and he thrusts his chest forward like a soldier about to receive a medal.

'Yes, a waiter . . . good, good. And your wife? You do have a wife?'

'I do, Comrade President. She used to be a train conductor.' The valet shifts forward in his chair and something shows in his expressionless face. Memories, perhaps, or embarrassment?

'Yes, a conductor, a conductor,' he repeats. 'She must have travelled a good bit of the world. That's what I've always wanted to do, travel a good bit of the world.'

'And your wish came true, Comrade President,' replies the valet, thrusting his chest forward again, as though he were responsible.

'We could have a look at what's going on in the world,' says the president. And while the valet glides cautiously towards the television, he sneaks a look at the bookshelves. The books are pretending to rest in their proper places, but he knows very well that nothing is easier than insinuating among those thousands of volumes one or two books equipped with a small peep-hole and a hidden device to bombard him with radiation. Sometimes, when he can concentrate perfectly, he can see rays of greenish poison molecules pouring out of the spines of these specious volumes and penetrating his head where they detonate, destroying his brain cells.

The television screen lights up, and the familiar voice of a familiar announcer intones: ' . . . and it's the correct way, the only way that will lead us forward . . . ' Someone applauds. Two men embrace each other, then one of them boards an aeroplane, turning and waving before disappearing through the door. But he is not one of those men, so he loses interest.

The valet returns to his chair and looks politely at the screen. 'Our society has never been closer to the great goals it has set for itself . . . ' the announcer claims.

The valet shifts slightly in his chair, and the president is suddenly worried that he might notice his lack of interest. He searches his face but sees nothing in it. 'Right,' he says. 'Right. And that's how it always is, today and tomorrow, for ever and ever. You can turn it off.' And when the valet turns towards the television set, the president takes another quick look at the bookshelves. One of the volumes moves almost imperceptibly, but he manages to glimpse the peep-hole in the spine of the book just as it snaps shut. The bier is still in the same place, but another one has now appeared beside it. Who is it for? For him, of course.

The valet walks back from the blank screen and sits down. His face expresses absolutely nothing.

'And how did you make a living before you came here, lad?' the president asks.

'I was a waiter,' he announces, almost proudly. 'I served food and drink.'

'I don't suppose you'd want to do that any more, would you?' he asked.

'I'm happy with what I'm doing, Comrade President.'

'You have a wife?' he asks him,

'I have a wife.'

'In good health?'

'In good health, fortunately, yes, in good health.'

'Not even a toothache?'

'Sometimes. She has trouble with her teeth.'

'And she has no other worries?'

'Only occasionally, Comrade President.'

'She shouldn't,' he says. 'Your wife shouldn't have any worries. Could we help her somehow, or do something to cheer her up?'

'I wouldn't dare take up your time with such petty matters, Comrade President.'

'Go on, speak!' he orders him.

'As a matter of fact, it would please my wife if you could look into a particular request for clemency.'

'Oh, my,' he says. 'Your wife is asking for clemency?

'No, I didn't mean that, Comrade President. My wife has in mind the one who hijacked the bus. The one they sentenced to death.' The valet's face remains expressionless as he conveys this astonishing request.

'But surely he wasn't her, or your . . . ?'

'No, no, certainly not.'

'Interesting, interesting,' he says. 'And why is your wife concerned about him?'

'Oh, you know women, Comrade President. She heard something, or maybe she even saw something, and took an interest. Besides'—the valet hesitates—'it's possible there may even be some distant relative involved here. You know women, they always have favours to call in.'

'Tell your wife not to worry about this,' he says. 'We shall take a look at the request.'

'Should I note it down for you?'

'Note it down,' he orders.

The valet stands up and walks over to the table. Now is a good time. The valet will write the note with his back turned, and he can slip out of the room unobserved and then escape into the garden. In the garden, in the farthest corner, he has a tree picked out, a plane tree, and all he has to do is shin up it. Its branches reach over the wall. Then he will jump—and be free.

Those boneheads thought someone might try to force their way in here from outside, so they cut down all the trees on the other side of the wall. It never occurred to them that someone, perhaps even he himself, might want to escape.

His breath quickens with excitement. He stealthily rises out of his chair, then, hovering above the floor, cautiously, very cautiously, he pushes off from the soft carpet and floats alongside the bookshelves. Then he sees him. Stuck into the shelves right beside the door, surrounded by thick volumes so that only his head and some parts of his incredibly twisted, misshapen body are visible, is his executioner. He recognizes him at once, those lashless, suppurating eyelids, that mouth full of yellowish-brown teeth.

So they sneaked him in after all. Their audacity knows no limits, even though they couldn't have been entirely sure of themselves, which is why they have packed him in so tightly, almost walling him in with books. Now the monster, surprised that he's been found out, attempts something meant to look like a smile.

What if he yells for his valet now? What if he goes to the telephone and calls a cabinet meeting immediately and declares a state of emergency? Then he'd be able to put this creature, and all the other ones as well, where they belong—in front of a firing-squad. But he won't do that. He has made a decision to rule without force.

'Comrade President,' says the valet's voice behind him, 'isn't it time to go beddybyes?'

He lands abruptly on the floor.

The valet helps him back into his chair. They sit facing each other again. On the other side of the bulletproof windows, deep night is pulsating.

He ought to stop drinking. His doctor recommended a strict limit of no more than two drinks a day. But who is this doctor, really? And who is this lad sitting across from him? He should ask him what his name is, what he did before he came here, if he has a wife and children.

But no matter what the fellow replies, it will all be a pack of lies.

CHAPTER TWO

1

THE DEMONSTRATION, WHICH was really more like a public meeting, had been given a permit. It was the first legal assembly of the opposition in twenty years. Most of the faces he saw through his viewfinder were familiar. They were the faces of those who had been branded as public enemies. That they were now standing on a podium addressing the crowd that had dared to gather was both a milestone and an unsettling omen. The authorities had allowed them to use a small square on the edge of the city. In a month or two, they would let them use a square in the centre, and if the demonstrators didn't get permission they would come anyway, so many of them that they would be unstoppable. You can rule with a firm hand, or you can rule through consensus. Those with neither the strength for firmness nor the courage for consensus take refuge in the belief that they can remain somewhere in between. But that is an illusion.

It was a freezing day. Clouds of breath were coming from the speakers' mouths, but they didn't appear to notice the cold. Even those who formed a circle around the podium had apparently so submerged themselves in the warmth of the words they heard that they were able to remove their gloves and bare their heads. Onlookers in the tenement houses around the square opened their windows to hear better.

There were many speakers, but Pavel was here today by himself. Sokol was off sick, and besides, his bosses felt it would be politically inappropriate to express too great an interest in this assembly.

Supposing he were to ask for an interview with one of the speakers? Would he be turned down, or would the speaker welcome the chance to talk to him? Probably the latter. These people had been denied free expression for too long.

What do you think about the state of human rights in this country? Does being allowed to hold this assembly represent a change for the better? Do you expect to be holding assemblies like this more often? What are your immediate aims?

But they would only be speaking to him. The tape would first be monitored by his bosses, who had expressly forbidden the conducting of such interviews. Would they fire him for insubordination? Probably. He shouldn't kid himself: just because they'd given in to these people didn't mean they'd give in to him as well. The people on the podium enjoyed an international protection of sorts: their names were known to foreign heads of state. His name was known only to the head of this state, that is, if he had taken note of it in the first place and managed to re-member it. By conducting such an interview, he would be helping neither himself nor anyone else. So why bother?

He filmed the speeches. He had to admit they were more interesting than the speeches of official politicians, and the faces of the speakers seemed more interesting as well. They were still full of expression and enthusiasm.

When he was packing up his equipment, an old man with a nose like a parrot's beak approached him. 'I see you're in films. What do you think about all this, sir?'

He shrugged. He had no desire to get into a conver-sation about anything, let alone this assembly, with a complete stranger.

'The voice of truth has been heard at last.'

The remark took him aback and he looked at the man more carefully. He was too old to be an *agent provocateur*.

'The truth can be silenced for years, sometimes for

centuries, but it will always come out in the end. Would you believe that I've been saying this for years now?'

When he received no reply, the man went on to explain: 'At first I told this only to my birds, but ever since they certified me, I say it everywhere. In streetcars, in bars, at meetings. I used to be a proper schoolteacher. First I had pupils, then I had birds in a cage, and now I have birds here.' He tapped his forehead. Then, with a dramatic flourish, he pulled out a dog-eared sheet of paper, apparently a certificate that confirmed his madness.

'Good piece of paper to have,' he told the old man. 'I'm sure it comes in very handy.' And he quickly got into his car to escape him.

An hour or so after dropping the tape off at the studio, he was climbing the stairs of an old tenement house only a few streets from the square where the public meeting had taken place. This was where he'd been born. He'd gone to school nearby. It was from this place that his father had run away. Then he too had tried to escape. Unlike his father, he had come back, and was still coming back today.

His mother was sitting in a deep armchair by the window. Now, in the autumn, almost no light came into the room. She was asleep. She seldom left her chair any more. He'd put the television where she could see it, but she never turned it on, nor did she ever open the book that lay on the table beside her. She could no longer sew; the needle was too small for her to hold in her fingers. Her life had become empty of interest. Her face was expressionless, and the veins on her hands stood out so starkly that they looked like a crude wood-carving. She reminded him more and more of a wooden puppet with the perfectly carved head of an old woman. One day, probably not long from now, he would speak to her, and touch her, and the puppet would no longer respond.

His mother shifted in her chair and looked at him through her thick glasses. 'Is that you, Pavel?'

'It's me.'

'What are you doing here?'

'I had some work nearby,' he explained.

'You're always up to something.'

'The opposition held a demonstration.'

'I don't know what you mean.'

'Some people gathered in a square. They made speeches.' It no longer made any sense to explain anything to her. She didn't understand him. Either she couldn't hear what he said, or she could make out the individual words but couldn't fit them together into sentences that meant anything to her. For years he'd talked to her about his life, mainly about his achievements, and she had listened to him. She'd been silent, perhaps even mistrustful, but she had listened. He found it hard now to accept the fact that he was losing her, that he had, in fact, already lost her.

'It's good of you to stop by. What are you up to all the time?'

'I finished that film about the president. They're going to broadcast it next month.'

She nodded. She had no idea which film he was talking about, nor which president. She'd lived through many presidents, and she wasn't interested in them. She wasn't even interested in him any longer. If she had ever been interested in anyone but herself, that is.

'What should I do?' she asked.

'We could go for a little walk.'

'I can't do that.'

'Why not?'

'Because I can't.' Then she added, 'It's cold out there.'

'You could take your coat.'

'I don't have a coat.'

'I'll fetch it for you.'

'I can't go for a walk when my feet are dead.'

Her feet were all right; it was her mind that was dead.

She closed her eyes. On a table beside her lay a plate of cold, half-eaten food—a few potatoes covered in a reddish-brown sauce with an unsavoury smell.

'What should I do?'

'What do you think you can manage?'

'I don't know. That's why I'm asking you.'

'Should I turn the television on?'

She didn't understand him. Besides, he saw that she wouldn't pay any attention. And anyway television was a sop for the lonely and forlorn, for people who see no one, to whom no one ever speaks. He took the plate with the leftovers into the kitchen. The washer on the kitchen tap was worn, and a thin stream of water dribbled out of it. Hanging on the wall above the sink, in cheap frames, were several photographs he had once taken: a self-portrait when he was eighteen, the hands of an old woman who by now was long dead. The Dalmatian in the next picture was dead too. He was called Ciudad. Ciudad means city. Back then, the word embodied all his longing for a far-away place. With this distant city in his mind he had planned his escape. When he was in prison, his mother used to visit him, always bringing a carefully wrapped parcel of food. On one of her visits he had asked her how she was. She had replied: What do you expect? I'm alone. Everyone's left me. Even you tried to leave me.

He threw the leftovers into the garbage and washed the plate. Then he fetched some tools and began dismantling the tap.

'I was fond of one person,' Albina had said to him when they had gone off to the borrowed cottage together. He waited for her to tell him more, but she said nothing and looked at him as though she had said too much already and now it was his turn to speak.

'Who was it?' he asked.

'It's not important. You didn't know him anyway. I only wanted you to know. We were going to get married.'

'But you didn't.'

'He left the country. He succeeded where you didn't. He didn't take the adventurous approach. Besides, he was older than you were then. He got himself an exit permit. Before he left he was able to sell almost everything he had. But he didn't tell me anything, and I didn't know until he wrote to me.'

'What did he say?'

'That we would meet again.'

'Do you want to meet him again?'

'Never!'

Her 'never' sounded very resolute. At the time he'd liked that, because her resolve had nothing to do with him.

'Where is he now?'

'I don't know.'

'When did this happen?'

'It doesn't matter. I don't know if I'll ever completely believe in anyone any more.'

'You will.'

'How can you know that?'

'I feel it. I can feel what is in you.'

What did he really feel? That she was a passionate being who was suppressing her own desires.

How long can you suppress your own desires?

Until you understand that in doing so you will destroy yourself.

'That's just talk,' she said. 'What can you know?'

'That I won't leave you.'

The same night she asked him: 'How can you do what you do?'

At first he didn't understand that she was talking about his work.

'You must know that what they broadcast is a lie. And you work for them. How can I believe anything you say if that lie doesn't bother you?'

'The two things have nothing to do with each other. I make films about animals.'

'Only about animals?'

'I like animals,' he said, avoiding a direct answer, 'and I don't have to lie about them.'

'I don't know. Maybe I don't understand.'

'I don't tell lies,' he said. 'I promise I will never lie to you.'

They had intended to spend the whole week at the borrowed cottage. They were together for five days, day and night. He wasn't used to that kind of closeness, and on the fifth day he was overcome by exhaustion, or perhaps it was anxiety. He felt trapped, locked in a cage, in a prison cell again, even though her tenderness made it easier for him. By the sixth day his need for change, for another voice and different company had become too great. He got up at dawn, when she was still asleep, and gazed at her face for a while. All at once it seemed alien and unfriendly. Her limp hair was stuck to her forehead, her sensual lips had become chapped and dry in sleep and marks left by his mouth were still visible on her slender throat. He tiptoed out of the room and fled, leaving not a whisper behind, only an unmade bed and an unfinished bottle of wine.

He ran across the dew-covered meadow and suddenly felt free.

What did it mean to be free?

It meant to have the right to define the space for our own actions.

Who conferred such a right?

We were born with it. He had believed that when he first tried to escape across the border, but they had denied him that right. He had let himself be deprived of it.

He finished fixing the tap, turned the water on and off several times and, when he was satisfied, he put the tools away, buttered a roll for his mother, made her tea and returned to the sitting-room.

'Did you bring me breakfast?' she said, surprised.

'Dinner. It's already evening.'

'What makes you think so?'

'Just take a look,' he said, pointing to a large clock on the wall.

'It always shows the same time.' His mother stared at the clock with a vague, confused look. 'A quarter to twelve?' she guessed.

'A quarter past five.'

'There's no difference. It's always dark outside.'

It was already getting dark and had started to rain when he returned to the cottage. He was drunk, drunk enough to walk jauntily, but not enough to be unaware of the wretchedness and the boorishness of what he had done. He saw the light in the window from a distance. She was still there. She hadn't gone, she was waiting for him. He didn't even know whether he was pleased or not. But at least he would have somewhere to dry his clothes and somewhere to sleep.

She was sitting on the floor, her knees hunched up under her chin, looking into the flickering fire. Her eyes were red from smoke, or from crying.

'Forgive me,' he said. 'I'm sorry.'

She was wearing black trousers and a shaggy white sweater with black horizontal streaks that made it look like birch-bark. She seemed beautiful to him, and he longed to put his arms around her. 'Forgive me,' he said again. 'I had to leave. I love you, but I had to see some new faces.'

'You don't have to explain anything to me.'

'I brought you something.' He reached into his pocket, but it was empty. All he could feel was a hole. 'Forgive me,' he said a third time.

'Why did you come back?'

'Because I love you.' He sat down on the bed and took his shoes off. 'I thought I'd be back before now, but I couldn't get away. There was this fellow there, he looked a little bit like my father.'

'Were you tired of me?'

'I guess I was.'

'And you say you love me?'

'I needed a rest. There's something strange and persistent about you. I can't relax beside you.'

'You don't need to explain anything.'

'Or perhaps there's something strange in me. I needed a change. I feel this need to escape whenever I feel hemmed in.'

'We can leave. Or you can leave by yourself, if you want.'

'No, it's all right now.' He stretched out on the bed. 'I'm glad to be back with you again. I just needed a break. You didn't feel anything like that?'

'If I had, I would have left too. Only I would have told you before I did.'

'I'm sorry. I should have left you a message. I didn't expect to be back so late.'

'I thought you wanted to stay with me. How could you stand being with me for the rest of your life if I bore you after a few days?'

'But that would be different. Here we were too alone. Too much together and alone at the same time.'

'Do you think that later on we won't be so completely together?'

'Well, there would be other people around, and then

we'd have to go to work. And there'd be children.'

Instead of answering, she began to cry.

'Why are you crying? Christ, why're you crying again?'

'You can go. Leave, if you find it hard to be with me.'

'I feel good with you.' He got up and put his arms around her.

'You'll always go away.'

'And I'll always come back.'

'If you still feel like it.' But she put her arms around him and began to kiss him.

That evening she told him for the first time that when she was little, her mother, who was a doctor, had been sent to India. She had gone with her, and they lived for almost two years in a city on the Ganges. One morning, she ran outside and saw a lot of gaunt people lying in the street. Then some men in dirty white coats came with a cart and loaded some of these gaunt men on to it. It was only years later that she realized those gaunt people were corpses. 'Sometimes, when I think about it, I can still see that scene so vividly.'

'What made you remember it just now?'

'Maybe because I feel a great restlessness in you. Mostly I remember that scene when I see how everyone around me is in such a rush, chasing after things they can't possibly find.'

'Does that mean you think I'd be better off dead?'

'Don't blaspheme. You know I want you to be alive. It's just that I'm afraid for you.' Then she said: 'You place too much importance on things, and too little on your own soul.'

'What is a soul?'

'It can't be put into words.'

'Well, how can I devote myself to something that can't be put into words?'

'God can't be put into words either.'

'I'm not saying I believe in God. Do you think the soul can be seen or somehow perceived?'

'I don't know. Why are you questioning me like this? You're making fun of me.'

'No. You're the one who started talking about it.'

'Indians say that the soul is woven from consciousness and spirit. From life and vision. From earth and water. From lightness and darkness. They say it's what is divine in man.'

'Is that what they told you there?'

'I had a teacher.'

'Do you think that animals have souls too?'

'Yes.'

'I'm glad. I don't like it when man thinks he's superior to the animals.'

Night was coming, and it was still raining. He got up and put some wood on the hearth. The fire smelled good.

He came back to her. They lay beside each other on the wide bed. Would he spend his life with her? Could he stand living side by side with someone for years?

'Do you feel claustrophobic here?' she asked.

'Why do you think that?'

'I feel that it's claustrophobic for you here. Should I open the window or maybe turn on the light?'

'Just stay. Stay here with me. I feel good like this. I like the dark.' He embraced her. 'Maybe I've been waiting my whole life for you, waiting for this moment.'

'Life is waiting for the light, not for the dark,' she said. 'My Indian teacher told me that. He was blind.'

'I'm already old, aren't I?' said his mother.

'Not that old,' he replied, as he always did. 'Others are older.'

'And how old am I, really?'

'You'll be seventy-eight next birthday.'

'I don't understand that,' she said. 'But yesterday they called me to the office and asked me whether I'd already reached my limit.'

'What limit?'

'Mine, of course. Seven thousand eight hundred metres.'

'What did you tell them?'

'That it's a pretty decent piece. It's such a big piece of cloth it can't even be measured. They wrote that down. They can measure very exactly. They have special instruments. They measure it and they cut it. That's what they're there for.'

'Should I read you something?'

'I don't know. What time is it?'

He got up. His books were still in the bookshelf. There were some novels and even several volumes of poetry. He'd got those from Albina. She'd given him poetry, but poetry wasn't his kind of reading. He couldn't concentrate on the lines or look for hidden connections between the metaphors.

He picked up a book from the little table. It was last year's Protestant almanac. He leafed through it for a while, looking for an appropriate text, but nothing caught his eye and so he began to read poems at random.

Then he looked into his mother's face.

She was oblivious.

Where is your soul, your wretched soul, your light, Mother?

2

HE STOPPED AGAIN at the studio to see his boss. Halama had already seen the tape. 'Good work,' he said. 'Obviously sympathetic. Maybe one day that will go down in your favour.'

'I just did it the way I always do. I can't control the expressions on people's faces.'

'It depends on who you shoot, and when.'

'There are faces you could look at for a year without ever seeing an intelligent expression.'

The boss laughed drily. 'Did you hand in all the tapes?'

He shrugged his shoulders.

'I know, it doesn't matter a damn. They had their own cameramen there anyway. I saw that video journal of theirs. Pretty soon we'll have two news broadcasts, two governments and two countries in one. Unfortunately, their video journal is better than ours. Not technically. But at least there's something to look at.'

'I could do that too.'

'Of course you could,' said the boss, 'if I didn't get in your way. Maybe you should work for them. It will count in your favour one day.'

'I don't need anyone to count anything in my favour,' he said angrily. 'Either I'm recognized for what I can do, or they can shove it.'

Halama had stopped listening. He rummaged through some papers for a while and then said, 'It looks as though they're going to loosen up, let us show more things now. Get some ideas together, put them on paper and we'll see.'

What is or is not allowed on television is mainly decided by Halama himself, Pavel thought. But he's only one card in a house of cards. Like me. One card goes and the whole house collapses. Doesn't he know that?

'I've got lots of ideas.'

'So, put them down on paper for me and submit them.'

'I think I'll wait a bit.'

'If you're sure they won't get stale.'

'Maybe just the opposite.'

'By the way, you're doing that meeting in the chemical factory. Think about what I've said. And if they get into a real discussion, try not to scare them. And since you're going to be there anyway, I've heard that people's lives are at risk in the aniline dye plant.'

'All our lives are at risk.'

In the flat he had been coming to for the past two years as if it were home, the woman to whom he behaved as though she were the mother of his son, although the real father lived behind the door next to their bedroom, was waiting impatiently for him. The boy was ill. He had a fever, and she couldn't get through to the emergency clinic on the phone.

'All right, I'll take him.'

'Are you sure you wouldn't mind? I don't know what else I can do.'

The boy lay in his room, his face flushed with fever. He tried to smile. 'We're supposed to be playing the last game of the season tomorrow.'

'You'll play in a lot of games yet,' he reassured him. 'What kind of an idea is this, to get so ill?'

'I must have got a chill during practice.'

'It's rotten weather,' Pavel said. 'And there's more crap in the air than a body can stand.'

As it turned out, the emergency clinic had a new telephone number (she might have thought of calling information), and the doctor had just gone out on her rounds. Robin's teeth were chattering with the fever, so he drove him to the hospital to save time. The hospital emergency ward was empty, and the nurse went to call a doctor. The boy sat leaning against his mother's shoulder. Eva stroked his damp hair. She clearly loved the boy, but what was her relationship with Pavel?

He was a man who slept with her and brought her money. He was a man who brought her money, and for that was allowed to sleep with her.

Whom did he love?

His father was dead and his mother was becoming a wooden puppet.

Where was Albina now? She might be only a few steps away. He'd have to walk over to the wing of the hospital where she worked. 'I'll wait in the car,' he said to Eva.

'You'll be cold.'

'I don't like hospital waiting-rooms. I'll turn the heat on in the car. Then at least we'll be warm on the way back.'

He would have time to go to the surgical wing. He would open the door, enter the brightly lit corridor and wait until the nurse came.

'Are you looking for someone?'

'I wanted to ask—a while ago there was a nurse working here, Valentová. Albina Valentová.'

'Albina? No, I can't say. I haven't been here long.'

'Of course, it was quite a few years ago. She must have left long ago. I just thought someone here might know where she was now.'

'Our matron might know. Or you could ask in the personnel department tomorrow. They should be able to help.'

'Thank you. I'll do that.'

Next day, in the cottage, it was still raining. 'I understand you,' she said suddenly over breakfast. 'When I was little and I'd done something wrong, Mother locked me in a cupboard in the basement.'

'Was that in India?'

'No, we were back home again by then. It was an

ordinary cupboard, but there were all sorts of bottles on the shelves and they seemed to be giving off light. I was terrified of those bottles. And I was afraid that a headless knight or some other ghost might burst into the room. I was too ashamed to shout but I cried and waved my arms to frighten the spirits away. Then I got the idea of closing my eyes and imagining that I'd escaped and was outside, in the garden, or the park.'

'It's good when you make up your mind to escape.'

'I could only do it in my head.'

'Could you do that now?'

'But I'm happy to be here with you.'

'We could run away together.'

'If you want. If it's too claustrophobic for you here.'

'What country would you choose?'

Eva and the boy came outside. 'It's pneumonia.' Eva looked terrified. 'We've got some antibiotics.'

'You'll be fine in a couple of days,' he said, stroking the boy's hair.

'You're so kind to us,' she said while he was driving back to the place he happened to be living in at the moment. 'We'll never forget this.'

3

ONE OF THE managing directors was waiting for them outside the main gate. The television vehicle couldn't go inside the factory grounds yet, he announced apologetically. The exhaust first had to be fitted with a protective wire mesh. Meanwhile, they could have a tour of the plant in his car. He could show them what they might eventually film, but he had to warn them that this amounted to practically nothing because practically everything was secret.

'We'll find something interesting,' Pavel said and he introduced his assistant, a man everyone called Little Ivens.

The iron gates were rusty, and a layer of white dust covered the ground. There was a sharp, acrid smell of ammonia in the cold air.

The manager opened the door of his car for them and warned the film crew that smoking was strictly forbidden throughout the plant. He hoped their cameras didn't give off sparks, he said with a dry laugh, and that their lamps would not explode. 'You know,' he said, waving his hand in the thick, stinking atmosphere they were breathing, 'sometimes all it takes is a spark.'

The manager was a man with a greyish complexion who tried hard to be jovial. He was a smoker and must have been miserable in a place like this. When they got into his car, he changed the subject to the reason he assumed they had come. They were being asked to elect a new executive director at the meeting, but everyone here felt that the old management team should be kept on despite the reforms. A large and important enterprise such as this one should be run by experts, after all. Of course there was a lot that needed changing. The equipment was antiquated, but that was not the management's fault. The enterprise had to pour money that might have been used to build a modern production line into the state coffers, and once the state got hold of the money, it simply evaporated, or rather got swallowed up by palaces of culture and power dams that did more harm than good . . . He stopped as though he had suddenly realized he didn't know who he was talking to, or rather, as though he knew exactly who he was talking to.

There were still two hours before the meeting began. On television, meetings were as boring as heads of state receiving ambassadors or saying goodbye to each other at airports. Unfortunately, this was precisely the kind of thing news producers wanted. They didn't care if viewers were bored or not. They knew that most people had no choice of programme and that they would look at the screen even if all they showed was smoke pouring out of smokestacks. Sometimes there were interesting faces at these meetings, but they were the exception, and they almost never belonged to the person who was speaking. The speakers usually had oddly shaped heads and spoke in slippery sentences. In the cutting-room Pavel's colleagues would often try in vain to find a single sentence that actually meant something.

The car bounced along the uneven road. The plant was laid out like a small town. It had streets, junctions, railway tracks and yard engines, hospitals, canteens, timberyards and its own signs with rules and regulations printed on coloured panels.

Pavel remarked that the windows in several buildings were smashed although the buildings were obviously still in use.

'Yes,' said the manager, 'even with the greatest precautions we occasionally have explosions. It's not worth replacing the glass.'

'Many dead?' asked Sokol.

'Oh no, not when you consider we're living under a volcano. Isn't it odd how people go on building their villages under volcanoes? We don't have a volcano of our own, so we had to make one.' The manager laughed stiffly. It was clearly not the first time he had delivered this witticism.

'Living under a volcano takes courage,' remarked Sokol. 'Building a volcano is just perverse.' A pity he would never say that on camera.

They stopped in front of a building that was newer and more modern than the others. The manager got out of the car to take them inside. Sokol was prepared to follow him, but Pavel was more interested in the place than in speeches, so he asked if he could look around the volcano.

The manager hesitated, and then moved to get into the car again.

'I can walk,' he suggested. 'In fact, I'd rather walk. You can't see much from a car.'

'But I can't let you wander around on your own. There are dangerous operations going on. I'm sure you'd like to take some shots around here, and I could probably arrange it, but not just now.'

'That's all right. I'll leave my camera here.'

'Good. Are you carrying matches?'

'I use a lighter.'

The crew followed the manager's interrogation with interest.

'You should have left it at the gate.'

'I won't light up.'

Looking slightly annoyed, the manager promised to send his secretary down to look after him, then went into the building. The rest of the crew followed. While Pavel was looking around the plant, they would set up the lights and position the cameras, which on his return he would order to be moved, just so they wouldn't begin to think him redundant.

He was alone. He noticed that most of the trees near the buildings had their tops lopped off. The buildings had roofs but they looked old and in need of repair.

A lorry carrying sacks and bearing a DANGEROUS LOAD warning drove by him. He could hear short, sharp detonations coming from somewhere in the distance. With every breath, he felt the air scraping his throat and making it hard for him to inhale. It would take more than sound and images to capture the stench of the poisonous fog that permeated everything.

Another lorry displaying a warning sign drove past, loaded with metal barrels. This plant was where one of the most effective plastic explosives in the world was made. It was odourless and almost impossible to detect, and every terrorist on earth was eager to get his hands on it. He wanted to see how they made it, but they would never let him, and if he so much as asked, they would report him for being too curious. How were they to know who he was working for?

The secretary finally came. They introduced themselves to each other, but her name was as ordinary as her appearance, and he instantly forgot it. She said she would show him what she could, even though there wasn't much: whatever was interesting was off limits. And there was nothing nice to look at.

'Do you make aniline?'

She nodded. She reminded him superficially of Eva. She wore thick make-up that blurred any individual features she might have had. She apparently liked purple, and she swayed her hips when she walked. 'But the plant is being rebuilt now. They had no choice. A lot of women ended up dead.'

'How many women work in the aniline dye plant?'

She gave him a look that suggested he'd asked her

something outrageous. 'Quite a few, a couple of hundred certainly. But they have to be at least forty years old. And they have to sign a waiver saying they understand what the consequences might be. To their health, that is.'

She took him into a warehouse and introduced him to a bearded foreman. The building was old. The walls had not been painted in a long time and were cracked in some places. Warning signs were displayed everywhere. An enormous ventilator roared up near the ceiling. Metal barrels were stacked neatly on spacious shelves. The foreman explained how they handled the explosives to avoid accidents. In the rear two women in coloured dresses were lifting barrels on to the highest shelves with a forklift truck. 'What would happen if one of those barrels fell off?' he asked.

The foreman grimaced. 'Well, they could spend a week trying to put you back together again but they wouldn't succeed.'

'It happens sometimes,' the secretary added. 'They find a watch on an arm but they can't find the body to go with it.'

They went outside again, and the secretary led him past some low wooden buildings. In the distance he saw a double wire fence and could hear the sharp crack of explosions coming from the same direction.

Suddenly he remembered the prison camp. Escape had been impossible, he couldn't leave for a day or even for an hour, he had nothing and no one, neither his camera nor his dog, nothing but his prison uniform, his defiance and his hope that one day all this would come to an end. He'd been certain at the time that as soon as he got out he would try to escape again, that he'd do it better next time and be done with this barbed-wire country forever. Instead, here he was, still around, waiting to film a meeting, a colourless, odourless, antiseptic meeting in rooms that reeked of death.

He looked around to see if there were guard towers and prisoners in striped prison uniforms, but he could only see two workers in blue overalls moving slowly in the distance, one of them carrying an iron rod on his shoulder. In prison camp they had cut iron rods, old, rusty iron rods, and sheets of metal. They put him into a gang with a man called Gabo, who was inside because he'd slept with his thirteen-year-old sister. Pavel hadn't given much thought to his crime; what bothered him most was that it was impossible to get Gabo to work properly, and because they couldn't fulfil their quotas, they had their already meagre rations cut back.

The explosions sounded closer.

'The dynamite plant is on the other side of the woods. They're always testing explosives over there. Do you want to take a look inside?'

'Will they let me?'

'They might, if I went with you.' She attempted a coquettish smile. 'You see those buildings in front of us? You can take a look in one of them if you like. You'll be surprised. Instead of setting up proper safety procedures and buying new machines, they simply put light roofs on the buildings. If there's an explosion, the roof flies off and so do the people, but the walls and the buildings around it remain standing.' She was becoming talkative, perhaps to reciprocate his own attempts to be friendly. 'Over there, in the nitroglycerine plant, they have fully automated vats for mixing liquids by remote control. But they still do it by hand, with paddles. The automated equipment doesn't work. If the men were to get slightly out of sync, they'd all go up. Have you seen *The Wages of Fear*? It's exactly like that. But no one's going to make a film about us. They'd never be allowed.

'I bet you're wondering why they work there. It's obvious: they do it for the bonuses. We're selling ourselves and we never think about it any more. Mum's got emphysema and she's on permanent disability. My brother's little girl is in the children's cancer clinic. In our block of flats three people have died in the past year and not one of them was over forty. Go to our cemetery and have a look at the dates on the tombstones. What good are bonuses to them now? But nobody thinks they'll end up that way. I'm the same.' She smiled flirtatiously again. 'But you'd better keep all this to yourself.'

The path led through the woods. There wasn't a soul around. If he were to put his arms around her now and kiss her, she probably wouldn't object, but what then?

Bare branches, trees with their crowns lopped off stretched towards the sky. The wire fence was quite near now, and he even glimpsed a soldier in a green uniform on patrol.

'Oh, look at the poor thing!' she cried suddenly. A jay was hopping about on the path waving a single wing in a vain attempt to fly.

The poor bird was being punished for the sins of others. Too bad he didn't have his camera with him. He would have liked to film the jay. A ghastly bird in a ghostly wood. If he ever made a film about the end of civilization, or about the world after some great catastrophe, the image might come in handy. But he would never make a film like that now. He would end up like this bird first.

He wanted a drink. He'd ask her to take him into one of the company canteens and buy her one to thank her for her company and then, then he would see. He really should have tried to remember.

She bent over and picked up the bird. 'Oh, you poor little thing. Are you afraid? Do you see that?' she said, turning to him. 'Do you see that?'

'It won't survive,' he said, 'unless you want to take it home.'

She shook her head. 'There's no point. I can't take them all home.'

'Let me have it.' He took the bird out of her hand and ended its suffering with a single twist. Then he kicked aside some leaves with his shoe, put the bird's dead body in the depression and covered it with leaves.

This factory, he realized, was a microcosm of the whole country: shabby, decaying structures surrounded by a double wire fence. Life is dying off, and not even the birds will survive, but there's something explosive in the air. All it needs is a spark, and everything will blow up.

Who will strike the spark? Who will survive the explosion?

'All the same,' she said, 'I envy you. By evening you'll be gone and you'll never have to come back.'

4

IT WAS SHORTLY after noon when he turned off the main highway and followed a road that rose gently through a wood. He still did not really know where he was going, but he needed to drive somewhere. He couldn't just stay put or return to a place where he'd persuaded himself he had a reason to be, where he thought he was at home.

Yesterday, when the meeting with the predetermined outcome was over, he had invited the secretary for a drink, and afterwards she took him to a party in a large house. Outside, to his surprise, several luxurious western cars were parked. Indoors, their owners were getting drunk. Though he drank a lot too, he was aware of how alien these faces marked by life under a volcano seemed to him. The secretary was pleased to have him as her guest, and she introduced him to people who had no desire whatsoever to know him, and whose names and positions he had no need to remember.

There were also many strikingly or scantily dressed women at the party, but they all seemed to be with someone. He listened to several stories from lives which, except for occasional explosions and premature deaths, were much like the lives people lead anywhere else. Here, however, the line between being and non-being had been blurred. Wherever this happens, other lines become easier to cross as well: lines marking greed, dishonesty, dishonour, shamelessness and the despair which probably lies behind all the rest.

What was greed, and dishonour? What was wretchedness?

Greed was a finger down the throat of the satiated, an extra room for useless junk, an unloved lover in one's arms.

As the night wore on, inhibitions vanished and, again without his camera, he watched a young man with trembling hands trying to give himself an injection, unable to find a vein. He saw a couple dance half-naked into the corner of a room and sink to the floor in an amorous embrace, and a man vomiting into a large Chinese vase through a cluster of red asters.

Dishonour was a substitute for honour which had exhausted itself in a vain attempt to bind someone to itself.

Then his attention was caught by a red-haired woman who appeared to be there alone. For some time now she had been gazing at him mistily. Her eyes were red, either from the smoke in the air or from crying. He invited her to dance. She shook her head, but then she stood up with great difficulty. 'Don't be angry,' she warned him, 'I probably won't be a very good partner tonight.'

'You mean a dance partner?'

'Isn't that all you want me for?'

'We don't have to dance if you don't feel like it.'

Wretchedness was the lot of those who hadn't the strength to be honourable nor the courage to be dishonourable. Wretchedness was the lot of those who, under all circumstances, remain in the middle.

She led him away to a room that was empty except for a solitary drunk who had fallen asleep in a leather armchair. She poured two glasses of cognac from a bottle that had been put there for guests who knew their way around. Five years ago, she said, she had married the marketing director of the company. She was a lawyer and had worked in his department. Her husband travelled a lot and had taken her on some of his trips. She had visited many countries and had seen a lot of exotic cities—Tripoli, Dakar, Amman, Lagos—but the names don't tell you anything. If you haven't been there, it's hard to imagine the atmosphere. The sea; the dark, narrow streets; hotels with swimming-pools on the roof; that strange light that makes everything seem to glow; those magnificent carpets in the mosques; the palm groves; the tiny villages with houses that look like brightly painted termite mounds; markets and bazaars where you can wander for hours, haggle with merchants and buy everything from magnificent embroideries, gold, precious stones and beaten copper to miraculous amulets, rattles, marimbas. You can't imagine those sounds, shouts, the music and the whistling, the different smells, and then evenings in sterile hotel rooms, negotiations in which millions change hands. You have no idea what an incredible demand there is in the world for a cheap explosive with no taste and no smell. They haggle over the price, of course, not like in the *souk*, but for millions. They stick envelopes into each other's pockets with cheques for amounts you can't even begin to imagine . . .

'Where's your husband now?'

'With some slut. Where else? He can buy any woman he feels like. He's thrown me off even though he pretends that he can't live without me. But he knows that he has to be careful, because if I wanted to talk about those business deals of his, nothing could save him, not even the fact that he's politically reliable . . . '

'Have you ever been afraid?'

'Afraid of what?'

'Of what you know.'

She shrugged her shoulders. 'The worst they could do is kill me. I have to die some day anyhow.'

But she didn't seem afraid to him. She was probably politically reliable too, enough at least to go on the record.

'Would you like to talk about this?'

'Maybe some day, maybe to someone, but not now, not to you.'

She knew the house well even in her drunken state. She found an empty room with a key on the inside, so they could lock themselves in. There were no couches, not even a bed, so they made love on the floor. She probably did it to get back at her husband who was big, powerful and rich enough to buy any whore he wanted.

Why did he do it? Because she was pretty and a little sad, because she had tried so hard to persuade him how exceptional she was, how far her experiences were beyond the reach of his imagination. And because he didn't know her name and because he thought he would never see her again.

He drove out of the wood and emerged on one side of a deep valley with a river winding through it. For a second, it flashed through his mind that instead of turning the wheel to follow the asphalt, he could drive straight on, and the car would fly off the road, Hollywood style, turn slowly over in the air and then plunge down into the rocks, the roar and crashing of metal on stone, the explosion and fire. The end at last. Going nowhere, expecting nothing, meeting no one, listening to no one, knowing nothing, bowing to no one.

From a distance, rising out of the autumn mists, he saw the castle where Peter was in his tenth year as caretaker.

For the first few years after serving their sentences, they saw each other often. They took advantage of a political thaw and started studying for their degrees by correspondence. When they got their diplomas, Peter, unlike him, refused to accept a position from which someone had just been dismissed. His religious convictions had something to do with his decision, and so did Alice, who shared Peter's faith. So Peter worked for several years as a linoleum layer, then he took a job as caretaker of a castle. The castle was not far from the place where they had both once tried to cross the border.

Peter could certainly have found more demanding work than looking after a nationalized, aristocratic country seat. But he wasn't complaining. He let it be known that his work gave him intellectual independence, at least. Neither baroque art nor the ideas of that period excited anyone any more. He could have had complete peace and quiet had he not taken up activities that the current legal system had placed outside the law. Both Peter and Alice wanted to remain independent: to associate with people, read books and live as they saw fit.

In a small village grocery below the castle he bought five bottles of red wine (they only had one kind) and three bars of chocolate for the children. He would have liked to buy something nice for Alice, but there was nothing here he could give her as a present.

Approaching the castle gate, he was stopped by a sudden, constricting pain in his chest. He had to lean against the wall. He should drink less, stop smoking, try to live his life differently. His job in television was wearing him down—not the work itself, but the conditions in which he worked. But what would he do if he decided to quit? He could probably make a living as a street photographer, but the right time for that had long since passed. He should at least take a rest. But where, with whom and, in fact, why?

He rang the bell. A window over the vestibule opened, and dogs began barking inside. A surprised female voice called out, 'Is that you, Pavel?'

'It's me, Alice, I was just passing by.'

The barking rapidly grew louder, then a key turned creakily in the lock. Two boxers burst through the door, jumped up on him and tried to lick his face.

'I just happened to be driving by,' he said.

'Where are you heading?' She was wearing a short skirt of printed cotton.

'I was on a shoot not far from here, in the chemical factory.'

'Way into the night?' she said, 'or right through till morning?'

'I suppose I do look pretty awful,' he admitted. 'I've been working like a dog recently, and I went on a bit of a bender.' He noticed that she too looked tired, perhaps even unhappy.

They walked together along a cold, gloomy corridor. Rust-stained engravings were hanging on the walls. She walked ahead of him. Her long legs had excited him the first time they met, and even after three children she remained slim, almost delicate. Her fair hair reached almost to her waist. Peter and he had met her together twenty years ago, when they were demonstrating against the invasion of their country by a foreign army. The foreign power had hypocritically presented its incursion as an act of assistance to help quell a non-existent enemy. They were standing near the radio building when they saw her, a girl in a short denim skirt and a boy's shirt, waving an enormous flag and shouting, along with others, the vain demand that the soldiers leave. Her eyes were dark blue. He'd never seen eyes of that colour before.

'They could start shooting any minute,' he had said to her.

'Why're you telling me this?' she said, 'I know it better than you do. They brought eight casualties in yesterday.'

They talked about those who had been shot, and about what would happen next. It went without saying that they were all prepared to take a stand, and even to die, but not a single shot was fired that day, and nothing happened to them.

Peter and he walked with Alice through the crowd and

down the square where years later, when he had learned to keep his own behaviour in close check, the demonstrators would gather again.

Strangers offered them refreshments, and they felt a special closeness that lifted them above the despair of the moment. That evening, they walked her home together. She lived in a hostel in the grounds of the hospital where she worked. They both kissed her goodnight. The kiss meant nothing, promised nothing. Still, he remembered it and he remembered her. He liked her looks and her personality. There was a warm-hearted openness in her behaviour, but beneath it he sensed hidden, impenetrable depths that drew him to her.

For a while they went out together, and he believed he loved her as much as she loved him. He was certain of this until something happened which, at the time, he thought far less a turning-point than she did. He preferred not to remember it now.

When they were going out together, Peter would often join them. They attended plays in small theatres or went to private screenings, which were a pleasure for Alice to watch and a duty for him.

He never stopped believing that Alice was more suited to him than to Peter, but later it became clear that she didn't think so. Or perhaps she sensed that Peter was more constant, more faithful and, most of all, more genuine. He missed his chance. Who might he have become had he been able to live by her side?

'Whether it was by accident or by design, I'm glad you stopped,' she said, smiling. She was always sweet to him, as though nothing had happened to sour their relationship.

They went up to the first floor.

'You'll have to wait a while for Peter,' she said. 'He's with an inspector from the centre. They're always nosing about. They'd love to find something wrong. Or at least to find something missing from the inventory. But they won't catch him out like that.'

'How will they catch him out?'

'They won't,' she said, and for a moment she looked almost annoyed. 'Peter respects the rules and only does

91

what's permitted. But as you well know, there are areas where almost everything is permitted.' Perhaps she suddenly regretted saying this because she added quickly: 'Even so, they won't leave him alone. Just last month they came to get him twice. They say they're from Criminal Investigations, but it's always the same people, the ones who are trying to drive us out of here.' As if trying to change the subject, she stopped in front of a door. 'Wait, let me show you something.' She unlocked the door, and he looked into a room containing several pieces of baroque furniture wrapped in sheets of translucent plastic. A fresco on one wall was disfigured by a layer of mould, and the parquet flooring was buckling in several places.

'They're trying to blame this on him too,' she said. 'At the end of the summer, a gale lifted off a piece of the roof, and we've been trying ever since to find someone to repair the hole. Peter covered it with tar-paper, but every time it rains the water gets in. It's a pity you're not a roofer. But maybe you can take a couple of pictures, and we'll send them to the ministry. Or you could make a film.'

'I doubt that they'd approve it.'

'I forgot, you have to have everything approved.'

'I can take some snapshots for you.'

He sat down in a chair facing the mouldy wall. The fresco depicted the birth of Venus. The goddess reminded him of the woman standing beside him, with long, golden hair tumbling down to her waist: he saw an infinite tenderness in both their faces. A big brown blotch was creeping down the wall, coming closer and closer to the goddess, threatening to swallow up her features.

A child was crying somewhere in the house. Alice had become distracted.

'Go and feed the children. Just ignore me.'

'You can come along.'

'I'll stay here. I'd like to take a good look at this mouldy fresco.'

He was alone. He could hear quiet music coming through the wall. The dogs were barking outside. What was he doing here? Why had he come?

Because he didn't have a home of his own.

He went from home to home, from castle to castle, like a wandering minstrel. Except that the minstrel had a lute and a song to offer. He had nothing.

What could a wandering photographer offer?

To take a picture.

A picture of what?

A picture of everything that could be captured on film: a hand, legs, clouds, snakes, banners, mouldy goddesses, presidents, faces, truncheons, naked bodies, flowers, hypodermic needles, fences, volcanic explosions.

What was a picture?

A picture was a motionless record of motion. An arrested representation of life. A picture was the kiss of death pretending to possess immutability.

What if he were just to leave quietly? After all, he had dropped in uninvited and he knew he didn't belong here. But where did he belong?

On a pile of old pictures.

He was lying to himself. He hadn't come because he was looking for a home. He'd come because he was looking for an alibi. One day he would be able to say: I was never ashamed of my friends. That is, if there was anyone to say that to. If anyone would listen. But he was still lying to himself. He was here because he needed, every so often, to see Alice.

Venus was looking at him tenderly. Her long blonde hair was waving in the wind, and flowers were drifting down around her. Suddenly he heard a stifled sob. He jumped. 'What's going on?'

Silence.

'Were you crying?'

Silence. A sob.

'Why are you crying?'

'You said everything would be different when children came.'

'Is that why you're crying?'

'But darling, what if they don't come?'

'We won't think about that now.'

'They won't come. I wanted to tell you anyway. You have to know. We would be alone.'

'What are you talking about?'

'If they came, it would be a miracle.'

'Are you sure about this?'

'I know it.'

'I didn't mean what I said about children. I never imagined I would have children. I used to imagine a lot of things, like being an Indian chief, but never that I would be a father.'

'You're only saying that.'

'I say it because I mean it.'

'But one day it will really get to you.'

'I don't know what will happen one day. Why should we think about it?'

Two months later Albina announced to him that she was pregnant.

Alice came to get him. She had changed into a dress of Indian cashmere, obviously for him. Perhaps she wasn't happy with Peter. Perhaps she hadn't been happy with him for a long time. Or she was bored with their quasi-exile. Something had happened between them, something that you don't even confide to a friend. But what kind of friend was he anyway? Chocolate bars for the children and the occasional visit couldn't hide the fact that he'd sailed away to another continent.

'They've left,' she announced, referring to a group of inspectors, whom he hadn't seen and didn't care about.

'That dress looks good on you,' he said. 'You're more and more beautiful all the time.'

'Thank you for saying so, but I know it's not true.'

Then he sat with her and Peter, his fellow escapee, his former partner in crime, in a small room in the castle. They drank red wine, and he tried to pretend that he felt a kind of closeness, a common bond with his friend, whom fate, or rather circumstances, had hounded all the way to this remote castle with mouldy walls and a leaky roof. Yet he felt neither closeness nor a common bond, just an uncertain sense of guilt, shame and envy. He needed to justify himself to Peter and even more to Alice. He told them about his problems in the department, where everyone was just waiting to pounce on everyone else's mistakes in the

hope of gaining promotion; about the director of pro-
gramming who flaunted her authority by forbidding women
to wear short skirts; about the chief producer who knew
that if he blocked a good piece of work, nothing would
happen to him, but if he failed to block something that
might upset a minister, or an under-secretary's wife, he
could lose his job and so, just to be sure, approved nothing
but ineffective and tedious mediocrities. Pavel's film on a
psychiatric hospital had been banned because it might have
been interpreted as an allusion to the country that ruled
over them, where they sent their political opponents to
such places. They even tried to block his film on carved na-
tivity scenes because they said it endorsed religious
sentiment. The film had taken almost a month to shoot, and
the commentary was written by an officially recognized
poet. Fortunately for the film, the official poet was very put
out by the ban and complained. The censor then ordered
him to tidy up the script. Instead of 'Jesus' he was to say
'the little child', and instead of 'the Virgin Mary' he was to
say 'the mother of the child'.

He didn't mention his ineffective and tedious film about
the president, which they had just finished editing.

He noticed that Peter was restlessly drumming his
fingers on the table-top. 'I can see what a bore it must be
to argue with the censors,' Peter said. 'But what I don't un-
derstand is why you hang on.'

Yes, faced with Peter, he had no defence, and should
never have mentioned his problems. At the same time
Peter's self-righteous superiority, which was possible only
because he had found a way to exist on the margins of
society, irritated Pavel. 'I got myself into it. Yes, I could
have tried working in some castle and waiting for things to
change. But I was afraid I'd forget how to hold a camera.'

'Aren't you afraid you'll forget where you are?'

'What do you mean?'

'I'm going to say this because no one else will. We
sometimes see your films. There's nothing to them except
a little technique. I mean, you must feel that yourself.'

'I do as much as can be done.'

'Exactly. And because not much can be done, you fool

around and kid yourself that it hasn't got anything to do with you.' Peter was frowning sourly.

'Are you saying I should have found myself a castle too?'

'What kind of question is that? You wouldn't dream of it. You have more important things to do. Like showing that anyone who dares to make a protest, or isn't completely happy here, is a criminal and a threat to the common good.'

If conversations like this had to happen at all, they should be private, between the two of them. But because Alice was here, Pavel said, 'I'm not trying to show anything of the kind. I can't help what they decide to broadcast. As far as the demonstrations are concerned, even if I sometimes get to shoot them, I'm never in on the final edit.'

'No, you just give them the material,' Peter said.

'Yes, but scissors can turn a demonstration against something into a demonstration for it, and vice versa.'

'Don't hide behind someone else's scissors. You must know when you're filming what someone is going to do with those scissors.'

'That's how it is. I can just mark time where I am, leave completely or turn material over to them and let them edit it. But I take pictures just like people do all over the world. I know that at least something of what I do will survive. One day it will make interesting documentaries.'

'One day, maybe. But people are watching this stuff now, and you're helping to mislead them.'

'So what? Do you think this is the only place where people are misled? Do you think that in other countries they churn out masterpieces? The minute you turn on the box over there someone's murdering somebody else or shooting them or kicking them when they're down. And those music videos! Once you've spent a few hours watching them, you're ready to believe that the world is a writhing, screaming, absurd madhouse. Of course you can always switch channels and watch a porn film or a horror show or look at piles of dead bodies, victims of the Mafia or terrorists or revolutionaries or brave soldiers who have just staged a *coup d'état*. And you can always find an ad that will tell you which chewing-gum brings the greatest happiness to the greatest number.'

'As you well know, I haven't had a passport for fifteen years and I can't make these comparisons as easily as you can.'

'That's enough,' said Alice. 'You see each other once a year. Do you have to argue? We all have our faults—it's just easier to see other people's.'

'Am I to take that personally?' asked Peter.

'It didn't occur to me that you would. But if you do, you probably have a reason.'

Just as another argument seemed about to erupt, one of the boys ran into the room and asked his father to come and help settle some less essential dispute, leaving Pavel alone with Alice.

'I don't mean to make excuses for myself,' he said, though in fact his greatest wish was to vindicate himself in her eyes, 'but I really did hope that I could do what I enjoyed doing and what I think I'm good at, and that people might occasionally learn something from it. And sometimes I think they do. Yes, I have to do things I detest. That's the price I pay. Almost everyone pays it, one way or another.'

'Peter only meant that you were destroying yourself. What you destroy in yourself can't be fixed, and that's not just true of alcoholic livers and smoked-out lungs.' Perhaps she wanted to add: or children killed before they are born. But she merely refilled his glass. He quickly downed his drink. They could hear children's voices coming from the next room. 'Would a little walk in the park help? I mean, since you were out drinking last night?'

The dry leaves rustled under their feet. The red of the honeysuckle contrasted sharply with the blue sky. She put her arm through his. The low sun surrounded her head with a shining halo. If only he could kiss her and hold her as he once had. But he knew that there was no point, so he merely said, 'It's beautiful here, and you are getting prettier and prettier. You seem to belong here for always.'

'Would you want to replace these statues with me?'

'It would certainly improve the park.'

'It would be fine during the day,' she agreed, 'but I'd be afraid at night. I don't know whether you heard about what happened. There's a club near here where the local big-shots hold weddings and banquets. One morning about a month ago, an escaped prisoner showed up with a machine-gun and killed everyone there. A cook, a waitress and three customers.'

'Why did he do it?'

'No one knows. Perhaps he went berserk, or perhaps he was drunk or just desperate. Or maybe he had always had murder in his heart and finally got his hands on a weapon.'

'Did they catch him?'

'They got him at the scene of the murder. He laid the corpses neatly side by side, then sat down, had a cigarette and waited. Actually, he must have been smoking two at a time, because when they found him, the ground all around him was littered with butts. The police just shot him. Anyway, I doubt they'd approve of me as a statue. They don't even approve your screenplays.'

'The fact that they don't approve isn't so important. I have screenplays ready that I don't even think . . . ' he stopped and then added, 'I think they're quite different.'

'Different from what?'

'Different from what I do now.'

'That's good,' she said encouragingly. 'Can they be filmed?'

He shook his head.

'Some day perhaps?'

He shrugged his shoulders. 'I don't know what will happen some day—or even if I'll still be around.'

'No one knows, only God.'

Now that he'd finally found the courage to mention his screenplays, he was disappointed she hadn't given him a chance to tell her more about them.

'But I believe that nothing this bad can last forever,' she said.

'Do you really believe that?'

'Yes. The world is like an enormous set of scales. When evil begins to outweigh good, angels cram themselves in on the lighter side. You can't see them, but there they are, restoring the balance.'

'You're that kind of angel, Alice.'

'Oh, you're always talking blasphemy. I believe in change because I don't want to stay here for the rest of my life. At least I don't want that for Peter. Actually, I quite like it, and the children love it. Growing up in a castle is quite different from growing up in some prefab high-rise. There's space here. Everywhere you go you can reach out and touch the past.'

Even the trees here were ancient. They must have witnessed many wars, many deaths, countless conversations. He noticed the imprint of a horseshoe in the sand on the pathway. Who could possibly go riding here?

'I'm glad you're not unhappy,' he said. 'People usually use their children as an excuse to explain why they are not living their own lives.' He wondered if he dared speak of himself as a potential father in front of her. Then he said, 'I think that if I'd had children, I'd be doing something completely different. Of course, you can only be decent for yourself. But you need to have someone, someone for whom you want to make the effort. I know that how I live is my own fault, but what good is it to know that?'

'You have Eva.'

He shook his head.

'OK, I'm sorry. But a person always has something more than just work and people he loves.'

'You mean God?'

'You don't think so?'

He shook his head. 'I don't see the slightest sign of his presence anywhere.'

'I'm sorry about that, Pavel.'

Now he ought to say: I am too, Alice. If I'd been able to see it then, our lives would have been different. But I could never believe that God was made man and let himself be crucified and then rose from the dead, or that centuries or thousands of years after my death I would rise again and return to my body to be judged for some actions lost in time. But it seemed absurd to talk to her about that. And besides, problems of dogma were not essential to her faith.

'When they tried Peter and me back then,' he recalled, 'they assigned me this old lawyer. When I got a year in jail, he told me: you're young, and it won't be easy, but you have to realize that what you can't avoid, you have to accept. There's no point in resisting the yoke. He told me that before the war, he'd been in America and watched them breaking in young colts on a ranch. The ones that resisted and bucked and kicked got beaten the hardest. At the time what he said made me angry. It seemed like a filthy morality he was preaching. But I've had many occasions to remember it since. I actually think he meant well.'

'It's a nice story,' she said. 'Except that we're not horses.'

FILM

I

THE MAN FROM the archives is elderly and unremarkable. He's wearing an army shirt, black trousers and grey shoes. Ella is dressed completely in purple because she knows purple excites men. Despite his greyness, the man does indeed give her a hungry look, but he addresses her politely: my dear Mrs Fuková. He listens to what she has to say with an obliging expression, but his grey eyes are crafty.

'Of course, I know his films,' he says. 'He was one of our best documentary-makers. Hardly anyone was a match for him in his field, but now . . . well, you understand.'

Ella is chilled by the little word 'was'. 'But he's not entirely banned,' she objects quietly. 'Occasionally they let him make something. He has the odd contract, but it's never the kind of film that lets him show what he can really do. It's very painful for him.'

'My dear Mrs Fuková, who said anything about a ban? No one is banned in this country. Your spouse is simply . . . shall we say, not in favour at the moment.'

'That's why I asked your wife. I just thought you might be able to arrange something. I understand you choose films for the president to watch. If you were to send him one of his films . . . ' Ella gropes for the right words. She's grown used to shady dealings in her shop, but even so, she feels oddly embarrassed and uncertain. Her husband—

101

who is not really her husband, and in whose interests she believes she is acting—has no idea that she's here. Still, she adds: 'We'd certainly make it worth your while.'

The man from the archives frowns, and she is suddenly worried. 'Of course, if you think nothing can be done, you can tell me straight out.'

'No, no, we'll think of something. I seem to recall your husband's film—from South America, or Mexico wasn't it?'

'Mexico.'

'Do you remember, Mrs Fuková, whether or not there's something in it about snakes?'

'Why, yes,' she replies eagerly. 'He did something on rattlesnake hunters.'

'Of course, now I remember. That's wonderful. We always send films about snakes to the Castle, mainly because the president's wife was interested.'

'But she's dead.'

'Comrade President maintains his old habits. At his age it's quite understandable.'

'Would you send him that film?'

'We'll try. Of course, that's not really enough. He doesn't pay much attention to credits any more. We'll have someone draw his attention to the director's name. And if he shows an interest, then we might point out that the director isn't exactly—how did we put it?—in favour at the moment.'

'And do you think you could arrange that?'

'For you, I'll do everything I can.' And he moves closer to touch her hair as a sign of his compliance.

'We'd be terribly grateful to you, and as I say we'll certainly make it worth your while.'

'Don't mention it, Mrs Fuková. My wife enjoys shopping at your store. She's always full of admiration at the way you manage to come up with everything she needs.'

She thanks him once again and promises to try and find something really special for his wife. Then she leaves, feeling that she has accomplished something that might win her the right to use the name by which the archivist has addressed her.

Fuka, meanwhile, is filming a news feature in a notorious chemical factory, which seems like a modern manifestation of hell. Because most of what they make here is secret, they show him the library, the showers, the clinic and a small timberyard between the buildings. They don't take him to the graveyard where the tombstones bear witness to the sudden deaths of young men and women— many on a single day. They introduce him to smiling female workers who speak in glowing terms of their miserable wages and their summer holidays in the company chalet. He manages to slip away from the filming and visit a building where workers are mixing an explosive liquid with large ladles in huge vats, aware that at any moment they might be blown through the roof, which has been specially constructed for this eventuality. He gazes in astonishment at this Boschean scene, aware of a gentle tingling in his spine, because his life too hangs by a thread.

When he returns to the crew, he finds someone else standing behind the camera, a colleague known to everyone as Little Ivan.

Little Ivan tells him he was sent over because they said Fuka had had to leave early. Someone has obviously got it wrong. Or, worse, no one has got anything wrong, they have merely decided to get rid of him.

Little Ivan reassures him that he has no personal interest in this job. It's hardly what you'd call a great environment here, and anyway he wouldn't want to complete a job that someone else has started. It's a question of principles.

Then why is he doing this?

What could he do? They ordered him to.

Fuka decides to call the studio management. By now he's convinced that there has been no mistake. True, he has a contract for this job, but what good is a contract in a country where the law is changeable and selectively applied?

As usual, he can't get through on the phone. He eventually calms down and decides what to do. They won't tell him anything over the phone. He'll deal with this in person.

The deputy director of the studio receives him in a friendly and even fatherly fashion. 'That wasn't really a job for you, with your abilities . . . ' he says, and Fuka begins to think that he was wrong, that something unexpected *has* happened, that a miraculous reversal has taken place. At last, they'd noticed his work.

'So what should I be doing?'

'You've made some interesting films. I remember the one about Mexico. That sequence about the rattlesnake hunters was brilliant.'

'I wanted to go back to Mexico, but you wouldn't let me.'

'Trips abroad are not my department.'

'*They* wouldn't let me,' he corrected himself.

'Others have to be given a chance too. You know how much a trip like that costs.'

'That film paid for itself. It was sold abroad.'

'No one's accusing you of anything. But you should try doing something like that here.'

'But you—they—turned down three of my ideas.'

'Is that so?'

'And I can't make a movie about rattlesnakes here.'

'Rattlesnakes are not the point. People are. You should find a good story.'

'You've just pulled me off something that might be called a good story. The conditions those people work in . . . '

'That's exactly what I'm talking about. You always look for the negative side of everything. That's not a good story; that's prejudice. I don't want to tell you what to think, but you know yourself that there are different ways of looking at everything.'

'I look at things the best way I know how.'

Their conversation continues. It is as round and slippery as a billiard ball. He can feel the phrases winding and tightening around his throat as though he is being enmeshed in a ball of string. He should start screaming but he knows no one will come to his rescue. What will he do? What should he do? Should he plead? Offer the deputy director a share of his fee? Walk out and slam the door behind him? How would he make a living? What would he have to live for?

He gets up and tries to smile. The deputy director smiles too and offers him his hand. His cuff slides up and Fuka glimpses the flash of a gold cuff-link. Or is he actually hiding a dagger up his sleeve?

'Don't fret,' says the woman he's been living with for two years. It's later in the evening and they are having dinner together. 'Even if they don't give you any more work, I'm still earning a living.'

Poor woman. Eight hours behind a counter for what he can make in one.

'It's not just the money.'

'I know,' she says, although what can she know? 'Today I went to see that man who works in the archives.'

'You went to see who?'

'I told you about it. The man who chooses films for the president to watch. He's going to send him your film. Everything will change, you'll see.'

'Oh, sure it will,' he says angrily. 'What did you do that for? Who asked you to go begging on my behalf?'

'You can't just let them drop you like that. And maybe the president will ask to see you. Then they'll come crawling, you'll see.'

He slams his fork down on the table. 'I wish you'd stop that idiotic talk!' He storms away from the table but has nowhere to go. So he turns on the television. A blue sky appears on the screen. There is a bright spot in it—an aeroplane. The aeroplane lands, a line of soldiers stands to attention. Another pointless visit. He should turn the damn thing off but he has to fill the time between dinner and sleep somehow. Then he sees him: a liverish face, fleshy lips parting to reveal sparkling white dentures. The dark, evil eyes behind thick spectacles stare ahead, ready to meet the new arrival.

The aircraft door opens. An enormous black man grins into the camera. The old man toddles stiffly toward the aircraft, followed by his sycophantic entourage.

Two men walk past the ranks of soldiers. Then the contemptible old man raises a bony paw to greet the invited guests, the sycophantic entourage and everyone who is watching television. Fuka gets up and angrily switches it off.

When he's lying beside Ella in the stuffy but immaculate bedroom she suddenly says, 'I've wanted to say this to you for a long time—if you wanted to have a child of your own . . .'

'What gave you that idea?'

'We've been together so long, how could I not have thought of it?'

'I know. Would you like to have another child?'

'I'd like to have one with you.'

'How nice.'

'What about you?'

'I . . . I've never really thought about it. You know the situation I'm in.'

'But you've been in that situation for as long as I've known you.'

'I haven't given it any thought for quite a while.'

'People have children in worse situations.'

'Yes. I used to think about it,' he added. 'It seemed odd to me that people would even consider bringing a child into a world like this. But I suppose that was shallow thinking. The world has always been a terrible place in one way or another.' He is spouting banalities—after all there have been times when he has enjoyed life and felt happy. 'I'll think about it,' he says, though he already knows he does not want to have a child with her. Then he embraces her.

They make love as they usually do: wordlessly, without great passion but deftly, both of them coming to a climax at the same time. Then she snuggles close to him and falls asleep almost at once, while he tosses restlessly on the bed, and in his mind caresses the woman with whom he might really have had a child, returns to the cottage where he stayed with her before leaving on his long journey across the sea.

Of course she doesn't go with him, and perhaps that's why she tells him about living in India when she was a child, and about the blind teacher who taught her about the human soul. They pretend that they are travelling in foreign countries, and are happy.

The rain that day beats relentlessly against the windowpanes, and the wind whips through the tops of the nearby oak trees. 'What country will you choose?' he asks Alina. Sometimes he calls her Ali, and sometimes Albina.

'I think I hear the sea. It's a warm sea. Even the sand is warm. And the mountains begin close to the shore.'

'Are they high mountains?' he asks.

'Not very high, but they look steep and bare. There's a pathway leading up into them. Do you see it?'

'Wait, yes, I think I do. It's winding among the boulders.'

'That's the one. There are shrubs growing beside it— tamarisk, I think. Would you like to see what it's like on the summit?'

'Why not? Perhaps we'll find something up there, something special. What sea is this?'

'It's a warm sea. When I was little I liked the name "Sargasso". It's the Sargasso Sea.'

'What's sargasso, Ali?'

'It's the name of a seaweed. It's brown.'

'For a long time I never saw the sea. After my attempt to escape, they wouldn't let me travel at all. Then I finally made it to the Baltic. The first day I climbed up on a cliff overlooking the water. I was lucky, because on the ledge of a nearby rock there was an enormous seal, sunning himself. The water in the sea was two different colours. A current, like a stream, was as blue as the sky, but there were dark currents flowing on either side. I sat there for maybe an hour, watching the pure waters battle the dark waters. I remember it well because it was unusual for me— just to sit and look. I was always in a hurry, always eager to see new, amazing things that would change my life.'

'Did you ever see anything that did?'

'If I did manage to catch a glimpse of something, I was soon past it. You can't find anything if you're in too much of a hurry.'

'You're not in a hurry now.'

'Now we're walking along a pathway that leads into the mountains. You know, I didn't really know how to look, either. I sought out things that looked interesting, that would make a good picture.' It seemed odd to be talking about himself so easily, without reserve.

And so on a rainy day, in someone else's cottage, he wanders through her landscape with her. They climb higher and higher until they near the summit. He looks around. The sea lies far beneath them and seems to rise like a smooth, shimmering slope to meet the horizon. The

tamarisk gives off a spicy scent. On a nearby rock a pur-
plish gecko is sunning itself. They climb through the final
twists in the pathway and come to a stony plateau over-
grown with high, yellow-brown grass which waves in the
wind. Perhaps this is sargasso grass. On the opposite hill,
several stony crags rise abruptly and barrenly to the sky,
heralding another range of mountains beyond. At the base
of one of the crags he can make out the shape of a white
building. Two low towers rise from a grey roof, and a
column of blue smoke hangs above it.

'What kind of building is that, Ali?'

'Perhaps it's a Buddhist temple.'

'Isn't it odd that it's the only building for miles? And
there's no sign of people.'

'There must be people there. There's a fire.'

'What if they're spirits?'

'Spirits don't need fire,' she objects.

As they get closer to it he begins to distinguish details of
the structure. There is an arched loggia running across the
front, and behind it several crenellated stone walls extending
back, punctuated by many entrances and low windows. The
steep roof is covered with shingle, and flag-poles extend
from the peak, with banners that snap in the wind.

'The windows are all closed, and so are the doors.'

'Yes. But there's someone over in the corner, sitting
under that little gable.'

'I believe you're right, Alina. He's wearing a black cape
and has long, white hair. He's sitting on a throne.'

'That's not a throne, it's a trunk.'

'Do you think he can see us?'

'His eyes are closed. I think he's blind. But he knows
we're here.'

'I have a strange feeling,' he says. 'It's as though I was
expecting something, as though I was about to learn some-
thing vital.'

'It will be him. My teacher. The blind one.'

'The one who told you what the soul comes from?'

'Yes.'

'He taught you about the soul. What else did he teach
you?'

'He taught me to exercise and breathe and concentrate and look into the setting sun. He also taught me how to disconnect from things around me and listen to myself, ask questions of myself and reply.'

'That's strange. I don't think we're getting any closer.'

'It's the air that does it. It's hard to judge distances, or . . .'

'What are you thinking?'

'Or perhaps we're not meant to meet him.'

'I'd like to know what he taught you. Would I understand?'

'I don't know. That would depend on you, wouldn't it?'

'I'll try, and you will help me. I'll be your pupil and you will be my teacher.'

'That's impossible. I can't be your teacher.'

'Why not?'

'Because I'm yours, but in another way.'

'But please, be my teacher, just for a moment.'

'All right. Shall we sit down here?'

'If that's what it takes.'

They sit down on the grass, which is dry and coarse. He watches the wind ruffle her hair. For a long time she says nothing. It makes him anxious. He also feels tired, close to exhaustion. Finally, he decides to speak: 'Why don't you say something?'

'Wait! You have to concentrate.'

'I see a bird of prey circling around the cloister.'

'Look at it but don't think about it. Don't think about anything. Slowly close your eyes.'

Silence. Her breath and the distant sighing of the wind. The whispering of the leaves. The rain.

'What are you thinking?' she asks.

'That you're near.'

'What is nearness?'

'There may be a definition of it, but I don't know what it is.'

'Try saying what comes into your mind.'

'I don't usually say what comes into my mind.'

'Say it now.'

'Alina, it's not easy for me to be intimate with someone.'

'That's exactly why I'm asking you this.'

'Nearness is the moment at which love climaxes.'

'And anything else?'

'I don't know. Perhaps the willingness to listen.'

'You're looking somewhere outside yourself again. What are you looking for?'

'I don't see that building.'

'Don't think about it.'

'It seems as though a fog has come in.'

'Don't think about it.'

'If the fog comes in, we might get lost.'

'Are you afraid?'

'Sometimes. Ever since they locked me up I'm afraid of falling into a place I can't climb back out of.'

'What is fear?'

'Fear is the touch of death, death reminding us of its existence.'

'Is death touching you now?'

'No, not now. It can't touch me when I'm with you, when I'm so near you.' And he feels something he never knew before—ecstasy, or perhaps true nearness.

The next evening he drops in at his regular bar. Little Ivan is here; he's obviously finished the job without being blown through the roof. The producer, Poštolka, is here too, and so is the crazy pensioner with the beak nose who used to teach history and natural science. He taught something he didn't believe for so long it befuddled his mind. Now he breeds exotic birds and is gradually coming to resemble one himself.

'I knew they were getting ready to shaft you,' says Little Ivan, looking indignant, though he had obviously not been indignant enough to turn down Fuka's job. 'I bet it's the police, because they confiscated your film. They put the word about, and now no one has the guts to let you work. You should definitely do something about it.'

It's the same advice he had heard yesterday from his woman. 'Actually, I couldn't care less.'

'What if they don't let you film any more?' Poštolka interjects; it sounds almost like a threat.

'But you brought it on yourself,' says Little Ivan suddenly.

'How did you work that out?'

'You made it too obvious you couldn't care less. You have a perfect right not to give a shit, but you don't need to tell everyone.'

'Or if you do, you've got to have the right piece of paper,' says the ex-teacher with the beak nose. 'Get certified or get a tame bird. My parrot can say the names of all our presidents, even the ones you don't have to say under your breath.'

'To hell with your parrot.' He takes a draught of beer. In his mind's eye, he sees a grove of mimosas populated by yellow-green parrots with coral beaks. Was he supposed to fly around in circles forever—condemned to live in an aviary from which only death could liberate him? He takes another draught of beer and waits in vain for relief.

Poštolka starts talking about a prediction he's heard about the impending end of the world. They say it will be the consequence of some cosmic catastrophe, but he believes the end will be brought about by people themselves. They will poison the earth and then, in a final gesture, blow it to smithereens.

As usual his opinions are second-hand and banal. The teacher with the beak nose pooh-poohs the predictions, then launches into a ridiculous account of the three possible attitudes a man who wants to remain free can take.

First, he can try to gain the confidence of those who have power over his career. He hides what he really wants to say in his most secret drawer, and puts his heart on ice. But he can never gain their trust, because those who have the power to decide his fate are untrusting as a matter of principle. Still, he may gradually make a career for himself; acquire a car; two women; and a cottage where he goes to make love, get drunk and forget. But the heart he has put on ice suffers, and the man will be prematurely struck down by a heart attack.

'Anyone who takes the opposite position,' the old man goes on, 'puts nothing off and gives no ground to those who have the power to decide his fate. So he keeps his integrity. But those above him never give him a chance, and he achieves nothing of what he had vowed to achieve.

111

Disappointed, he takes to drink, and will probably end up in a clinic.'

The third position is somewhere in between. He dissimulates, makes concessions to the powerful, while at the same time secretly trying to live and work in harmony with his beliefs. Yet he knows what he has done wrong, and because his heart is still in his body, he torments it with pangs of conscience for so long that he eventually breaks down. He will probably end up in an institute for nervous disorders. An Austrian writer has claimed that before you can do good, you must first impress people. The old man, however, claims—with the air of one offering him the flower of his wisdom—that man must first do evil in order to gain room in which to do good, if he is still capable of doing good.

The old man's ranting angers Fuka. 'Shut up!' he shouts. 'Save the advice for your budgies.'

The bar closes at eleven o'clock. The producer invites Fuka to go on drinking. The former teacher invites him to visit his aviary. Little Ivan promises to put in a good word for him. He certainly means it, at least until he sobers up.

Fuka walks unsteadily back home along an empty street. He notices a drunken woman sprawled on the pavement opposite. Her handbag is in her lap and she is wearing a kerchief. She's probably from the country.

'I just couldn't make it,' he says to Alina when he returns, 'I had the air tickets, but there was an earthquake. You must have read about it.'

'I know,' she replies without looking at him. 'But I was desperate to have you back. When you didn't come, something happened, something inside me.' She'd lost some weight after the occurrence. She was wearing a yellow kerchief and not a hair on her head was visible. She must have had it cut.

He takes out snapshots showing half-demolished houses, the ruins of a bridge, crushed cars, uprooted trees, sunken pavements, cracked walls and cracked earth and even dead bodies arranged in a row beside a pile of rubble. 'It was spooky,' he says. 'I've never experienced anything like it. You don't really know what's going on. If you could hear an explosion or something—but there was only the sound of things cracking and then shouts and then a moment of silence and then the cracking sounds again, and everything's trembling and you still don't know what's going on. I ran out into the street and at that moment the first building collapsed . . . '

She shakes her head, not wanting to hear any more. 'I'm not accusing you of anything,' she says. 'Something happened, and I don't love you any more. It might have happened even if you'd come back. You're different from how I imagined you, from the person I'd like to live with.'

He wants her to tell him how he is different, but she suddenly begins a strange fit of trembling and begs him to leave her alone, never to call her, never again, to forget all about her.

He is dumbstruck, but he manages to nod. He wants to kiss her one more time. He takes her head in his hands and kisses her cold lips. He smells the perfume of her breath, but she does not reciprocate the kiss and tries to wriggle free of his grip. As she does so, the kerchief slips off her head, and he's stunned to see that she has lost not only the child, but her hair as well.

Fuka pulls his camera out of its case, and he even manages to change its lens and photograph the drunken woman, who may or may not have hair but almost certainly has no home to go back to.

What is a home?

A home is something we carry inside us. Those who do not have a home inside them cannot build one, either from defiance or from stone.

II

HE FINISHES HIS breakfast. Since his wife died he has breakfasted alone. Alone in spacious dining-rooms, at enormous tables spread with bright white tablecloths, served with generous portions of food he hardly touches, for in the mornings he suffers from a feeling of fullness. But he must take a few mouthfuls to help him swallow all the pills his doctors have condemned him to take. The nurse, or his faithful maid, always lays them out on a tray beside his glass of milk. They wait until he's put each pill into his mouth and swallowed it. Only then do they wish him a pleasant meal and withdraw. Sometimes he manages to hide some of the pills under his tongue or to shift them into the space between his teeth and his lips and then, when he is alone, he spits them into his glass of milk. But how can he know which of the pills is beneficial and which contains the slow-acting poison they are feeding him to ease him gently out of this world? How can he, when he doesn't even know which of his doctors is real and which merely one of his many executioners in disguise?

He slides his chair back from the table, gets up and walks across the soft carpet to the window. The harsh noonday sun is pouring into the garden. Two men are running a coloured bundle of cloth up a pole. He waits by the window until the bundle reaches the top, breaks open, and fills with wind. He's certain that he's never laid eyes on that kind of flag before. Two goats, or perhaps they're antelopes—at that distance it's hard to tell—face each other on a green-and-white field.

That's the sort who come to visit him. They embroider their flags with goats, elephants or monkeys and they expect him to embrace them, smile at them and be photographed with them. He should look at the map to see exactly where this president of goats comes from.

Sometimes these potentates bring him acceptable presents: lion skins, an interesting weapon, a dagger with an ivory handle or a rifle with a finely carved butt. When his wife was still alive, they would bring her magnificent fabrics, embroideries, ostrich-feather fans, shawls that she could wrap around her whole body, hairpins set with precious stones. Those who were better briefed would bring shoes or handbags made of snakeskin.

He feels like taking a look at some of those old gifts. He leaves the room and walks down an inner staircase to a hall, where he waves away a valet and goes into a room with a high, panelled ceiling and wood-panelled walls.

This is where he keeps both the gifts he likes and those he doesn't care about, gifts whose worth he cannot even guess at and gifts whose value, if any, is symbolic.

Here are glass cases crammed with marble ashtrays, boxes with mounted butterflies, busts of himself, folk carvings from the Cameroon, peasant costumes, a leather saddle from Mongolia, a grandfather clock, crystal goblets, cut-glass chalices, Chinese vases, Japanese plates and also some models: miniature machines and motors, automobiles, rockets, aircraft, spaceships, models of his residence, of factories and blast furnaces, dams and television towers, models of weapons, and, of course, real weapons as well, hunting guns both antique and modern. He stands for a while in this odd junk shop, his very own flea market. He opens one of the cases and takes out a bronze plaque and a diploma bearing an enormous seal. He stares at it for a while, ignoring the obsequious citation in which his vassals, all men of letters at a famous university, award him an honorary doctorate. Then he returns the piece of wrought metal to its bed of velvet. He leaves via the rear doors set almost invisibly in the panelled walls. He walks along a narrow corridor until he comes to a side staircase. He goes down the stairs to another room, in which the windows are covered with ornamental grilles, and the ceiling is vaulted like that of a wine cellar.

This is his room. The walls are white and bare, with no pictures or decorations, only shelves that hold his special collection of strongboxes arranged in rows. These are treasure chests, but they are empty. No coffers could contain his wealth; the entire country belongs to him. Their only value for him is that they can be opened and closed again, that he can admire and investigate their complex, precise mechanisms. Sometimes he pretends to himself that he's lost the key to one of those apparently foolproof boxes, and he has to try to break into it using the methods he was taught by the safe-cracker he shared a cell with when they were both in the hands of the executioners. Not with a blowtorch, in that barbarian way they do it in gangster films, but with fine wires and files.

Of course he collects locks as well. Brand-new locks;

locks with rusty works and complicated systems of levers that operate huge bolts; modern locks in which miniature springs trip small steel-tongues with teeth, and gears that mesh to create apparently solid elements; locks that can be opened with keys, or by setting the right combination of numbers on a dial, or by slipping a card with a magnetic band or a pattern of punched holes into a narrow slit on the face of the mechanism; locking devices that can only be activated by using the right five keys. There are combination locks in which a key can only be inserted after the proper combination is dialled, locks which trigger sirens the moment the wrong key is slipped into them. All these devices thrill him and allow him to forget his ceaseless flow of worries.

Sometimes, when he has the time to linger, he isolates himself completely from the world that surrounds him. He sits down on a round stool. In front of him, on a workbench, are boxes with labels in foreign languages, new and as yet unwrapped packages sent to him by faithful embassy employees. They understand next to nothing, of course, and they usually spend large sums of money buying out the first junk shop they come to—or sometimes they even buy them in a department store.

Impatiently, he tears the wrapping off the first parcel. A golden padlock tumbles out of the box. At first, it looks like an ordinary lock, but he cannot find the keyhole. He explores the lock carefully with his fingers. The box will certainly contain a set of instructions to help him find the opening mechanism, but he derives great satisfaction from discovering how these things work by himself.

Sometimes he imagines himself changing the locks of his residence during the night. Then he will summon the impostors that swarm around him—the doctors, the valets, the gardeners, the bodyguards, the ministers, the chauffeurs, the cooks, the secretaries and the waiters—and invite them all into one room. He will then excuse himself, leave the room and lock them in. He will also lock the door in the hall and the gate at the main entrance. Now, let them call for help, or telephone out, or shout through the window; let them break down the doors. But before they manage to raise the alarm, he will have walked freely through the gate and vanished into the forest, and it will be a day or two before they find him.

He hears footsteps in the corridor and quickly puts the lock aside and looks guiltily at his hands. They are smeared with oil. He wipes them and then holds them behind his back.

The valet appears in the doorway. 'Comrade President, the Comrade Chancellor has arrived,' he says, his face expressionless.

'Let him wait.'

'In two hours, you must be at the airport. The Comrade Chancellor urges you . . . '

'I know. Let him wait.'

They never give him a moment's peace. They have sophisticated ways of harassing him, of wearing him down. And just now, when he was ready to begin work. 'Let him wait!' he repeats. Let them all wait, including the nigger who doesn't care about meeting him anyway. All he's interested in is women, or what he might be able to squeeze out of them. They call it extending credit. Credit extended to eternity, and never otherwise. Everything we do here is forever, and meanwhile death knocks on the armour-plated gate.

He walks heavily up the side staircase.

In the library everything is spotless. Not a sign of yesterday evening. He remembers sitting here, but who was he with? They've done this to him deliberately. Whenever he drinks a little, they always remove the evidence of what he did, so he can never find out what happened, never know who he talked to, about what. On the writing-table they have arranged his briefing papers, as they always do. On top of the pile is a small note written in an unfamiliar but legible hand:

Dear Comrade President,
As you requested, allow me to remind you that you wanted to see the director, Mr Fuka, whose film about the rattlesnake hunters in Mexico you enjoyed.

There was no signature, of course. Who could have

forged this? Who is leaving him messages like this without having the decency to sign them? Unless the person assumed he would recognize his handwriting, or remember asking for a memo. He does have a vague memory of something like that.

He opens the folder and finds another message.

Dear Comrade President,
If you'll allow me, it was your express wish that I remind you to consider the request for clemency submitted on behalf of the hijacker Bartoš.

Again, no signature. This is beginning to annoy him. Someone has infiltrated his study and forged these shabby little memos. Now that he thinks of it, though, he does have a dim recollection of a film about rattlesnakes. He remembers a scene in which some half-naked savage was holding a repulsive snake in his hands. As he watched he thought of his poor wife. She would certainly have been fascinated and would have wanted to invite that native to see her. But why was he expected to grant clemency to a director? Had the director stolen something? Or had the snake bitten him? Had he not come home, and then changed his mind and wanted to get back into the country? Such things happened. Hadn't a well-known singer had the same problem? He had simply telephoned him and told him all was forgiven. But then he remembered another criminal who had hijacked someone. He would never dream of pardoning him.

The memos were probably slipped into his papers by his mortal enemies to confuse him and then trap him.

He closes the folder again and then suddenly, he remembers. The valet! Yesterday evening his favourite valet was sitting here with him. But why would he be concerned about the life of some criminal elements? Evidently, he was only passing on someone else's request. All over the world, there was always a tremendous outcry whenever one of his sworn enemies ended up behind bars. How concerned they all were about who was in jail! They even protested when ordinary criminals and murderers were locked up. That's what really irritates him about these self-righteous critics: they invoke the law in regard to those who have never hesitated to break it. He knows these criminals: he has shared prison cells with them and paced concrete prison courtyards with them. They can't tell him these people are innocent victims.

He's incensed. As if he didn't have other things to worry about besides the lives of a few nobodies. As if violence had never been perpetrated on others. As if they had never sentenced anyone to death themselves. And what do you have to say, gentlemen, about those sixty miners lost underground, or those five hundred women working in the aniline dye factory who are gradually dying of cancer? Someone should stand up for them. But what can he do when the world pays good money for those dyes? All his ministers and his bankers, all those people who are just waiting for him to make a wrong move, would pounce on him at once for depriving the state of the necessary dollars.

But they don't hesitate for a moment to bring him those poor wretches covered with white shrouds. Like those little babies: how many have they already brought him, and how many are yet to come? He doesn't know. In the northern coal basin, every eighth child is born dead, and soon it could be every fourth child. All those poor little creatures who died from inhaling that terrible smog saturated with poison. Who stood up for them? Who sent protests in their defence?

All these unfortunates could have submitted requests for clemency. They were the true innocents, but they didn't ask for a reprieve; they did their duty. They were simple working people, heroes, patriots, waiting silently for someone to stand up for them.

The learned minds in the Academy of Sciences are predicting a day when a sufficient supply of energy can no longer be guaranteed. A freezing day when the generators in the electrical plants give up, and the trucks that bring bread to the cities won't start, and people don't go to work and are trapped, imprisoned in their freezing homes with nothing to warm themselves with and nowhere to run to. All they will be able to do is put on their overcoats and rush into the streets, where they will loot the shops and rampage through the cities in mad terror and rage until they come to the Castle, where he will still hold power, and they will demand that he feed them and give them warmth. He will live to see a time when he can no longer show himself to the people whose welfare he has desired, whom he has served for so many years, because he will have nothing to offer them but the end, nothing but slabs of wood on which to lay out their dead.

People everywhere are waiting for someone to stand up for them, to fulfil both their hidden desires and public demands, to fill their stomachs, house them, provide them with heat and light and water and air, grant them clemency and guarantee them a feeling of security forever, but his powers are only human, stretch them as he might. And he's surrounded by enemies, imprisoned among pretenders who doggedly wait for him to make the fatal mistake, wait for his fall, wait for his end.

And they dare bemoan the fate of a violent criminal!

Thank goodness there are still people to be found who can take his mind off these things. Like the fellow who made the film for him about hunting rattlesnakes. One of the rattlesnakes reared up and rattled and blinked its tiny eyes, just like his chancellor. He should command the chancellor to watch the film as well. Let him see it. Let him learn something.

The chancellor waddles into the room, little snake's eyes, the legs of a chicken, a leonine mane smoothed smoothly back, large protruding ears. 'I suggest we speed things up, Comrade,' he hisses with his snake's voice. 'We must depart soon, in an hour.' And he gestures vaguely towards the leather folders.

The chancellor carries on talking, dispensing advice and instructions. A walking textbook, this treacherous rattle-snake with the legs of a chicken. The capital city is Omba (or Bomba—he didn't quite catch it, and it's beneath his dignity to ask). They can offer us uranium, cocoa beans, cotton and copper; the prime minister studied law at Cambridge, even if he is black, from the Bantu tribe. Now be careful: the Bantus have an ancient culture, they even have their own literature, epic poetry. Avoid mentioning law; talk about the economy instead. Remember they give us uranium, copper, cotton, cocoa beans. We give them trucks, cannons, tanks, chemicals. Don't say anything against God, avoid ecclesiastical politics, music is a possible, the prime minister plays the piano, is fond of the romantics—Grieg, Beethoven, Wagner, Tchaikovsky, Liszt. Stay away from modern painting in our own country. Advisable to talk about the struggle against colonialism. The prime minister has a special custom: once a month he has a complex court case presented to him, along with appeals and petitions for pardon. He summons the disputing parties, hears the case himself, offers his opinion or grants clemency as the case may be. This practice has won him acclaim both among his own people and abroad. He has suspended the death penalty, so it's advisable to avoid mention of our own practice.

And then there was the recent accident at the explosives factory. A while ago, when a whole building blew up, he had ordered the management to take strict measures to avoid a recurrence. Instead, they merely rebuilt the roofs so that when an explosion did occur, the roof would blow off and the walls would remain intact. Of course there was another explosion, and they all went through the new roof—the nitroglycerine mixers, the entire saltpetre section, eight fifteen-year-old apprentices, the warehouse workers and a car park full of lorries and drivers and drivers' mates—all of them lifted into the air in a single instant, transformed into ashes and smoke, atoms of human matter scattered in all directions by a whirlwind. Not a single recognizable particle of any of those people was ever found. The officials were refusing to issue death certificates, and the president would have to intervene personally, visit the place himself and put medals in the hate-filled hands of weeping widows and angry widowers and, in this way, confirm the deaths as heroic, the victims as heroes of labour, as warriors in a common cause, the cause of the people, of the most forward-looking system in history, for which so many have already laid down their lives.

When he awoke that night, there were the biers again, covered with white sheets. This time there was no one under the sheets, only emptiness, air. He got out of bed and walked past them, opened the door into the long corridor, and there they were, more of them, side by side, each with a white sign at its head with a name written in black letters. A hundred and thirty-nine of them. And when he walked past them, down the corridor faintly illuminated by the moonlight, the biers suddenly began to float. He couldn't understand how his enemies had created this effect. Perhaps it was overheated air, or magnetism, but the biers floated up to the level of his chest, wobbling slightly so that the wooden legs and the frames collided and sounded like the clacking of bones, like a menacing applause, and then, above all these sounds, there emerged a high-pitched howling, as though a hundred throats were wailing all at once, and he came close to opening the window in sheer terror and jumping out to escape those sounds. He might have leapt from the heights into the depths and fallen, not flung to his death at the hands of an outraged people but driven by the intrigues of those who did not hesitate to exploit the wretched victims of a tragic accident in their silent campaign against him.

And the prime minister's wife—he realized that the cunning reptile was still speaking to him—her name is Patricia, she's his only wife, and be careful to remember that both are Christian, she studied psychology in California and you can talk about charitable activities and medical care, not about . . .

The valet enters carrying his black suit over his arm. He will tell him that the time has come to go into the bathroom and change. The chancellor snaps the folder shut. 'Any comments, Comrade President?'

The ministers and experts will be present at the negotiations. Let them worry about those things. That's what they're paid for, after all. Let them think about something else for a change besides their secret Swiss bank accounts.

'Would you like to read over the welcoming speech now?'

'In the car, there'll be time enough in the car.' The valet guides him into the bathroom.

There's a shirt on a hanger, a pure white shirt, and his

golden cuff-links lie ready on a small wooden tray.

Suddenly he has an idea. 'That hijacker, the one sentenced to hang,' he says, turning to the chancellor. 'Do you know who it is?'

The chancellor does a little skip on his chickenlike legs and nods enthusiastically.

'Summon him here,' he orders. 'I want to hear what he has to say.'

'But, Comrade President,' he says, winding himself around the president's leg, 'He's a dangerous criminal and the court has already sentenced him . . . '

'Summon him,' he repeats, 'I want to review his case and offer an opinion.'

'Of course, Comrade President.' The chancellor's voice sounds constricted, as though the hunter were already closing his hand around his neck. 'When?'

'Find some time,' he says. 'But let it be when this nigger is still here.'

'Yes, Comrade President.'

'And that film-maker who entertained me so well.' The name has slipped his mind and he doesn't even know the film-maker's crime. That's not important, they'll find that out for him. Let the chancellor look at himself writhing in the hands of a hunter, watch as they break his poisonous teeth.

'Should I summon him as well?'

He dips his hands in the wash-basin. Behind him the valet obligingly holds a clean white towel ready for him to use. The chancellor's snakelike eyes gaze at him disapprovingly.

That's their method: prevent him from meeting with anyone, except perhaps some black man who will put on airs and flaunt his authority. They even say he can act as a judge because he's got a Cambridge education, while the president has only been to a provincial university. So he will choose someone, summon him and then demonstrate his magnanimity. But how can he do this when they sabotage his invitations, when they only pretend to do as he says? And then, of course, they spread rumours that he can't relate to people, that he's incapable of judgement, of making decisions, that he can't do anything, or change anything and should therefore be replaced. But he will surprise them all. He will foil their treacherous plans, and one day, when they least expect it, he will appear before the people and declare freedom. Let the people themselves decide his fate, and then let all his enemies tear themselves apart. But he will have done what he had to do, and no one will ever again say that he lost touch with the people or that he had governed merely through compulsion and fear.

'The day after tomorrow at the very latest,' he orders. 'And bring both the criminals here in a civilized manner. I don't want to see any shackles, or any handcuffs.' He sighs and begins to pull his shirt over his head.

III

IT'S EIGHT-THIRTY in the morning. Once again, a key rattles in the lock at an odd time. With the guard in the doorway are two unfamiliar men, one, obviously some big-shot, in uniform, the other a fat slob in civvies with a pistol swelling his back pocket. Could this be the moment?

Robert rattles off the regulation response with Gabo's quickened breathing on the back of his neck.

'Bartoš, get ready to go!' The guard's voice sounds strange; it wavers, with a tinge of kindness in it. It fills him with a terrifying premonition.

'What about my things?'

'Did I say anything about things?'

They lead him down the stairs without even putting the cuffs on him. He doesn't know what to do, so he counts the floors as they pass them. As they approach ground level, his terror intensifies. The steps lead directly to the exit into the third courtyard. Maybe the gallows are down there ready for him. They will drag him on to the platform and some shit-faced strangler will push forward, probably this fat guy in civvies, and yell at him to prepare himself. It's only now that he can imagine what it will be like. He can't stop visualizing a pair of huge, hairy, sadistic hands fingering his throat. He can bite them, at least, kick the bloody sadist in the balls, and then they'll jump on him as

they have so often before, only this time will be the last
time. There are always enough of them to overpower him,
and then nothing in the world could prevent those dis-
gusting hands from tying the noose around his neck.

Sweat pours down his forehead, and the back of his
shirt is soaked. Aren't they even going to offer him a last
breakfast? Won't they let him smoke his last cigarette?

They walk past the exit to the courtyard and trudge
down the stairs into the basement. If they were to shove
him into a bunker he'd go quietly. Anything would be
better than the rope. That would put an end to everything.
They go past a row of bolted doors until they come to one
that's open. Inside, a guard with a simian forehead brings
him civvies, and he is ordered to change. Then they herd
him down some more corridors to the barber's shop where
a man in a white smock sticks a paper cloth under his
collar, soaps his face and passes a razor over it a couple of
times. At one point, his chin is in a tight grip; the barber
would only have to make a quick slice and that would be
it . . . But he doesn't. The barber rinses his face off and
even sprays it with some kind of perfumed shit, and then
they can go.

Why hasn't he ever wondered about how they would
play the last dirty trick? He might have realized that these
bastards would have their pleasure spoiled if they had to
watch a jailbird swinging in shit-filled sweatpants and a
vomit-stained windcheater; that's why they're decking him
out like he's going to a wedding. Finally, at the end of the
corridor, they put the cuffs on him. A grille slides back and
he finds himself in the first courtyard where two policemen
and a yellow-and-white prison van stand ready. The po-
licemen escort him to the wagon, but before they can
shove him inside, someone in civvies rushes up gesticu-
lating wildly and says something to the fat man. Then the
fat man goes over to the driver and sends him and his
rabbit hutch on wheels to hell.

So they just leave him standing there and it's more than
he can take, so he turns to one of the escorts and asks him
where they're taking him. He knows he won't get an
answer, but even to be yelled at would be some comfort.

But nothing happens. They remain silent, deaf to his questions, and that terrifies him even more. If they were to start beating him now, he might not even have the strength to defend himself. He'd just howl like a dog drowning in a flooded river.

Then a black limousine pulls up. The fat man gets in beside the driver, he's put in the back seat between the two escorts and they drive off. The gate opens, and soon they're on the open road.

He hasn't a clue where they're taking him. Why are they wasting petrol? Maybe the gallows are somewhere else. Or maybe one of those sadistic bloody hangmen didn't feel like coming all the way out here, so they sent this limo to pick him up. They're giving him a last ride instead of a last meal. If this is going to be his last ride, this is also his last chance to make a run for it. If he could only get out of the car, he'd manage the rest.

The idea blinds him like a flash of lightning, and he has to hold his breath in order not to shout. He knows he mustn't move or make a sound, otherwise they'll get scared and handcuff him to the escorts. So he pretends to fall asleep, while from under his half-closed lids he watches the cars coming from the opposite direction and the roofs of houses and church steeples passing by. They're doing at least ninety. It will be enough to mangle them all to mincemeat. But he has nothing to lose.

Mentally, he rehearses the movement several times until he's sure he can pull it off. They are just coming out of a wood and approaching a small town. He hopes that this is not their destination. He can't put it off any longer. He mustn't be too choosy. He can't afford to hesitate, or they'll get him to a place from which no prisoner has ever escaped.

They drive through the town, then into the countryside again. It's straight out of a film, farm ponds sparkling in the sun, surrounded by trees. It's quiet in the car. No one speaks; the escorts merely glance at him occasionally. The car roars down a hill, through a wooded area. Below that, he can see that the road curves to the left, but it's not a sharp turn; the driver probably won't even brake. All he has to do is choose the right moment. Sunlight flashes through the trees. A huge lorry is bearing down on them. His throat has gone dry. What hope does he have? At this speed? He reminds himself he has nothing to lose. He flings himself forward and with all his might, like a football player lunging to head the ball into the goal, he head-butts the driver from behind. He hears a cry of pain, some cursing, someone pulls him back but then lets go, there's more shouting and he hits the floor, his hands helpless, but he braces himself with his legs, feels the car leave the road, feels the first impact and then he too shouts, with fear or joy, the car flips over, a crushing impact. Darkness suddenly cloaks his eyes as he hears the shattering of glass and cries of terror and pain.

He tries to lift his head. A reddish, spinning light penetrates the darkness, and he can see the vague outline of things, people, which become more distinct: a twisted door has been punched in on its frame and has pinned one of the escorts to the seat. The dead eyes of the second escort stare up at him from a bloody face. With his hands still cuffed behind his back, he manages to raise himself and shift to an opening between the frame and the door. He sees the driver draped bloodily over the lifeless body of the fat man, but he hasn't time to think about it. He squeezes through the opening and is out of the car and taking his first free step. He feels a piercing pain in his left leg. Surely the fucking leg can't have taken the impact, not now when he needs it most. A car is coming down the road. It will probably stop. They mustn't see him with the cuffs on, so he tries to run. It's almost impossible. There's a pain in his abdomen, his leg is probably wrecked. Fiery wheels spin before his eyes, blood streams down his face, his face is probably messed up too and he can't even wipe it, but at least he's moving, not like those motherfuckers, he's moving, gradually dragging himself into the trees, and he even tries to run, groaning with pain under his breath, but he's running.

He has no sense of time, but when he finally looks around, the road is out of sight.

He kneels down and wipes his head on a pillow of moss like a wild animal. When he gets up again, the moss is brown with blood.

In the distance he can hear the wailing of a siren. It could just be an ambulance, but it could also be the police. They'll bring dogs, and then how long will it take to track him down?

He begins running again, if you can call this painful, stumbling limp running. Everything depends on how soon they realize he's escaped and how far away he is when they do.

The woods are not deep, and he suddenly emerges into a field of wheat flooded with light. The field slopes away into a valley where he can see several damp, glistening roofs. A narrow, dusty path runs alongside the field. He limps down it. It would probably be better to hide among the wheat, but as long as they're not on to him he has to get as far away as he can. Beyond an orchard, the first house appears, and he looks around cautiously. As far as he can tell, there's no one outside in the sticky pre-noon heat. A few dogs bark lazily.

He walks past three houses, and in the yard of the fourth, a fair-haired boy is kneeling over a dismantled bicycle.

He shouts at him and as he does so, his face contorts with pain.

The boy looks around and then gapes. He can't be any more than twelve.

'Are you alone?'

The boy gets to his feet. 'What is it?' he says, and backs warily towards the door. 'What do you want?'

'Can't you see? I need help.'

'Yeah, I can see.' The boy stops. 'Did you fall?'

'That's it. You by yourself?'

The boy looks around in alarm. 'Me and the dog. What have you got behind your back?'

'Just my hands.' He turns round to show the boy. 'Look, I won't hurt you, I just need help.'

The boy calls the dog, a limping old mutt that would be hard put to scare a chicken. The two of them edge towards the gate. 'You've run away.'

'You've got to help me . . . ' Every word he utters is painful, and his mouth is so dry he can hardly move his tongue.

'My brother has a blowtorch in the shed,' says the boy, and he unlocks the gate.

Inside the shed it's dark and cool, and there's a smell of hay. If he could only lie down. The boy quickly unwinds the flex, puts on the goggles and ignites the torch. 'Are they after you?'

'Shut up and get on with it.' Then he thinks again. 'If they turn up here, asking questions, you never saw me and you don't know anything about me.' He pulls his wrists as far apart as he can, but he still feels the heat of the flame. 'They can't do anything to you. You're not fifteen yet. But even so, you never saw me. If they keep on at you, say you were indoors.' The handcuffs are beginning to get hot but he grits his teeth and keeps his hands apart.

'OK,' says the boy. 'What did you do?'

'Best for you not to know, but I'm innocent.' At that moment his hands fly apart. The steel bracelets still hang on his wrists, but he can get rid of them if the boy will give him a piece of wire or a penknife.

'Do you want to have a wash?'

The first thing he does when he reaches the wash-basin is drink, gulping down long mouthfuls of water. Only then does he look in the mirror. He can scarcely recognize himself. His hair is matted with blood. His right cheek and upper lip are swollen. His left cheek has been cut by glass.

The boy is standing behind him. 'My brother was in jail too. He deserted from the army.'

He wets his hands in the water and carefully runs them over his face. 'Remember, you haven't seen me!'

He sticks his head under the tap. The sharp sting brings tears to his eyes. He reaches for the towel, then decides against it and merely takes another drink.

Meanwhile, the boy has found a large pastry. If he asked him, he could probably dig up some cash as well, but he probably shouldn't waste any more time here. He can always get money. He limps across the yard to the gate.

He should clear out of this village as quickly as possible and perhaps try and find a car, though they must have blocked all the main roads by now.

He hobbles along the fence with his head down. Not a

soul anywhere. People are either hard at work somewhere or swilling beer in the bar on the square. Parked in front of it—this really is his lucky day—is a lorry. The village square seems deserted, and he reaches the back of the lorry without being observed. He lifts the canvas flap. There are cases full of bottles inside. He bangs his wounded leg as he swings himself over the tailgate, but he grits his teeth and doesn't utter a sound, lands on his haunches and pulls the canvas shut behind him.

The bottles are empty, another piece of luck, because it means they won't unload them until they get to the brewery. The cases are not heavy, and he rearranges them so that he's surrounded. Now if they'd just get out of here. The police could arrive any time—if they've managed to figure out that he's escaped.

Then he hears voices. Someone lifts the canvas and slides a few more cases of empties inside, then the doors slam, the motor starts and the vehicle drives off.

If only he could see where they were going. But at least he's getting further away. Every minute, the circle they will have to look for him in is widening. Unless they're taking the bottles right back to the town where they put him in the car that morning. The lorry rattles over the rutted road, and the bottles clatter. They've probably begun the search by now. The police will have been alerted. Maybe they're even sending in helicopters. It won't be easy. Once he gets out of this lorry, he'll have to find a hostage. A woman. At least one. He won't be as naïve as Míla was and let her go. He won't even negotiate.

At that moment the lorry begins to slow down. Robert sits absolutely still and listens to the voices coming to him through the canvas.

Your papers, driver.

Where are you coming from? What are you carrying? Have you seen a man in a dark suit, probably badly wounded, wearing handcuffs?

A voice mutters some reply.

He hopes they don't have those trained dogs with them, but even if they did, he doubts they could pick up his scent over the strong smell of beer.

A shaft of light penetrates his hiding-place. They must have lifted the canvas.

The motor is still running, which is a good thing because it will drown out his breathing. Someone thumps the side of the truck. They move one of the cases. Then silence. They probably don't feel like shifting all of them. He knows them well enough to know what lazy bastards they are. They wouldn't bother, unless they had a whole platoon of prisoners to do it for them.

The lorry starts up again. He's beginning to believe he'll make it out of here, out of this mess, out of this shitty country. He only has to be tough. No mercy, no negotiating.

Now they're moving fast. The driver is obviously in a hurry. Then the lorry slows down, begins bumping over a cobblestone surface and finally comes to a complete halt. He hears the creaking of a gate opening, voices, the lorry inches forward, the motor coughs, then dies. The doors slam, and someone jumps to the ground.

He has to stay on his toes. If they start unloading the bottles, he'll have to come up with a way to get out of here without being seen. But what if he can't? He gets up, still hidden by the barricade of cases, tries to flex his arms and legs, then pulls an empty bottle from the top row of cases, gets a good grip on it and waits.

But no one comes. He can hear a woman's voice some-where nearby. Someone is dragging something metallic over the cobblestones and whistling. Then silence again. He's probably wasting precious time in here now. He puts the bottle down as quietly as he can and starts shifting the crates to one side. He crawls out of his hiding-place and carefully lifts the edge of the canvas.

The lorry is backed up against a loading ramp with wooden doors. In front of the doors there's a tall pile of the same kind of cases that sheltered him in the truck. He climbs cautiously on to the loading ramp and looks out from behind the truck. He is in a cobbled courtyard with a set of rails for a yard engine running across the middle of it. High brick buildings dominate the courtyard on two sides. The third side is formed by a stone wall with a gate-house. The fourth side appears to be the best place to hide, since there are only a few one-storey buildings, apparently warehouses. He can't see anyone; the working day must be over. He creeps cautiously along the loading ramp towards the low buildings. When he passes the last of these, he comes to an open area that serves as a scrapyard. It is filled with rusting machines, old pipes, bundles of wire, piles of empty tin cans, used barrels and even a few ancient, rotting beer wagons. Behind that, there is an overgrown wall low enough to crawl over. Beyond the wall are three apartment blocks, the only vantage point from which he might be seen.

On a pile of refuse he finds several pieces of wire and nails, then he squeezes under one of the old wagons. It will be hard for anyone who doesn't know where to look, or who doesn't have a dog, to find him here. He can remove the handcuffs at his leisure.

He begins to probe the lock on the handcuffs. He's managed to open other locks before. Even back when he was in the children's home, he was determined not to become a uranium miner or a mason. They'd threatened and cajoled, but they backed off in the end and let him train as a locksmith. He'd learned by then that you have to know what you want and let no one stand in your way.

The spring clicks, and he shakes the hideous mark of imprisonment off his wrists, squeezes out from under the wagon, walks over to the pile of scrap metal and throws the handcuffs into an old barrel.

He's not afraid of work. If he lived in a decent country and could open his own workshop he would happily work twelve-hour shifts every day; he would be his own boss, not someone else's lackey. Occasionally, he would close the business for, say, a month, pick up some cute little thing and take off with her to somewhere where they would all call him 'Sir'.

He goes back under the wagon and pulls a flattened and somewhat stale piece of pastry out of his pocket. It's getting dark. Where are they now? There isn't a sign of them. He's given them the slip. If he had some food, he might be able hold out here for a few days. Meanwhile the police would get tired. They'd realize they'd lost him. His leg would have begun to heal, his whiskers would grow and by the time he got himself some new clothes those smart-arse bastards wouldn't recognize him, not even if he flagged them down and hitched a lift.

But the only thing to eat here is nails washed down with stale beer. And tomorrow morning, people would start turning up for work, so by then he'd have to be somewhere else. His best chance would be in some ordinary house where he could wait for a day or two by himself or, even better, with a hostage. But he has some time now, and he can afford to take a rest.

He stretches out on his back and stares up at the underside of the wagon. A clump of old dried clay is hanging from the mud-covered boards. He closes his eyes and tries to ignore the pain in his leg. It seems to him that the wagon is beginning to float above him slightly, that its floorboards are becoming transparent and penetrable. He passes through them and gently rises above the earth, floating higher and higher, like a kite. When he's so high that not even the sharpest eye can discern him, he catches the wind and floats west until he can feel beneath him that cursed line, defined by barbed wire, so impossible to cross on the ground.

CHAPTER THREE

1

TINY FLAKES OF snow swirled in the air, melting the instant they touched people's clothes. The crowd was so densely packed that almost no snow reached the ground. Carrying his camera on his shoulder, Pavel pushed his way through the people until he reached the statue of the country's patron saint. They had hung flags on it and surrounded the saint with flowers and burning candles, and stuck posters on the pedestal demanding free elections, democracy, the end of one-party rule, dialogue, freedom of expression and information, the dismantling of the People's Militia, solidarity with the students, a general strike and the resignation of the government. Only a few days ago no one would have dared voice a single one of those demands, let alone write them down and post them up in the centre of the city. And even if someone had dared to do so, the poster would have disappeared before anyone had had a chance to read it.

The demonstrations had been going on for five days now. On the first day, the police had attacked a student march with such fury that they had wounded many of the participants and onlookers. How many had really been hurt, he didn't know, nor did anyone else. Official reports could not be believed, many of the wounded were afraid to seek medical help and doctors preferred not to reveal how many they had treated. Either the cruelty of the police had gone beyond bearable limits, or the present regime's time had simply come without its even noticing. The students declared a strike, were joined by actors and supported by everyone Pavel knew from earlier demonstrations, and this time they in turn were supported by all those who had so far remained silent. There were so many of them that only gunfire could have scattered them now.

He watched with amazement, or rather with suspicion, this strange transformation by which those who had so recently been beaten and doused with jets of water now addressed the assembled crowds, and those who had until recently been silenced and bowed now cheered, clenched their fists, raised two fingers in the victory salute and rattled their keys in anticipation of victory.

What was victory?

The illusory hope that a dream could last; the mad dance of those who are about to die, on the graves of those who have just died. It was a state in which the weeping and wailing of victims was drowned out by shouts of joy.

In the faces of people, he saw an ecstasy that he had seldom witnessed.

He looked around for the familiar faces but could not see them. The people who filled the square now had obviously swarmed out of places he had never been. They were an alien people, yet he found their excitement infectious, to the point where he had to remind himself that he was here to record the event, not to join in. If anything excited him, it should be the possibility that what he was filming might actually reach television viewers. For the past two days he'd gone around with Sokol, who had suddenly become a man of action. He forced his way into striking schools, tirelessly asking people questions without trying to second-guess their answers as he always had in the past.

And now Sokol was thrusting the microphone into the face of a plump older woman. He had selected, perhaps unconsciously, a type he chose to interview during the May Day celebrations every year. 'What do you do?' he asked her.

'I work on a cooperative farm.'

'Great! And what exactly do you do there?'

'I milk the cows.'

'So you've come from far away?'

'I have a daughter studying here. It's not right for them to beat our children.'

People gathered round to listen.

'It's enough what they've beaten into us. They hauled my father off to the uranium mines. Do you know why?' She was getting ready to launch into her life story. But now wasn't the time for life stories. Pavel panned his camera into the crowd where a little boy was perched on a man's shoulders waving a flag.

He could hear chanting down the square: 'We want truth! We want truth!'

The little boy shouted something too. His voice was lost in the swell of other sounds, but he seemed to be joining in the chant.

What was truth?

Sokol had now turned his microphone to a young man in blue overalls.

Until now the belief had been that truth was what you found in the pockets of workers' overalls, under miners' helmets and in the heavy gloves of steelworkers.

The young man announced that his workmates in the factory supported the students. He'd come here to demonstrate for genuine socialism.

What did he understand by that?

Justice, free elections. Not to have the police beating innocent people. The right to travel.

The demonstration was almost over. When he was carrying his camera to the car, he finally saw a familiar face, and smiled broadly. 'Alice, what are you doing here?'

'Surely you didn't think I'd be sitting at home at a time like this?'

They walked together down the square. The crowd was gradually thinning out.

'Do you remember that time, long ago, right here . . . when we first met?'

'Yes. It was far more hopeless then. That was the beginning of the darkness.'

'Do you think the light is coming now?'

'You don't think it is?'

He shrugged. 'I have almost no time to think now. We're filming from early morning into the night. As a matter of fact, I haven't had a thing to eat since breakfast.'

She put her arm through his just as she had twenty-one years ago, except that then there were three of them.

They found an empty table in a small restaurant just below the square. A television in the corner of the room was still showing the demonstration. 'You've done a tremendous job,' she said, gesturing towards the television set. 'People who can't come to the city will learn what's really going on.'

'Did you leave Peter at the castle?'

'I haven't seen him for about three days. He simply vanished. He's in meetings somewhere.' She didn't seem anxious to talk about him.

'What about the children?'

'They're with their grandmother. We're taking turns. It's her turn to come here tomorrow.'

'You're being very responsible about it.'

'But there's so much at stake,' she said. 'It's about how we're going to live from now on. If we lose now, we'll lose the opportunity for years to come. You don't see it that way?'

'I told you, I don't have time to think.'

'You're making excuses, Pavel.'

'You say "if we lose". Who are "we"?'

'"We" means all of us, doesn't it?'

'All the people can't lose all the time, and all the people can't win all the time either.'

'It would never occur to me to look at it that way.'

'I'm not looking at it any way. I'm only saying that usually some win and others lose. Sometimes it turns out that the ones who lose are those who thought they had won, and vice versa.'

'You're being disgustingly objective about this, or at least you're pretending to be. Doesn't any of this concern you?'

The waiter put two glasses of wine on the table. 'Will you be leaving your castle now?' Pavel asked.

'Probably. If all this works out. But to tell you the truth, I can hardly imagine leaving. And anyway, I asked you a question: what about you?'

Why was she asking him? Was it out of interest in him? Or was it rather with a sense of malicious satisfaction that now it would be his turn to suffer for a change?

'It does concern me. Don't you think I want to work freely? What I don't know is: will I be able to work freely if things do turn out well?'

'Do you think you've lost the knack?'

'I hope not. But what if the winners decide to include me among the losers? What can I do then?'

'You're talking nonsense. You'd finally do what you do best and you'd do it the way you wanted to.'

Perhaps she was genuinely interested in him after all.

'If only. If only you were making the decisions.' He paused. 'It would be nice. But I can scarcely imagine it myself. I haven't even thought about it much. I'm not in the habit of thinking ahead. I've spent so long up to my neck in the present. It was like a spider's web with a lot of spiders in it, not just one. They lay in wait for you at every corner of the web. Once you got caught in it you couldn't get free. And they didn't suck your blood right away, they'd just very slowly wind you into their web: they'd approve this, censor that, come down on you for showing something that shouldn't be shown, or for not showing something that should have been shown. They'd involve you in meetings, briefings, political training sessions where you were told how to work by people who'd never done anything in their lives. If you told them what you thought of them, you'd be fired on the spot. Sometimes I thought I couldn't take it any longer.'

'But you took it.'

He nodded. He still wanted to find a way to vindicate himself in her eyes. He explained that the world could not be neatly and clearly divided by a line that separated good from evil, that separated him from her. 'When I was in Mexico we got to see a television studio,' he said, recalling an incident that had brought this truth home to him. 'They showed us their fantastic equipment. Their network is well endowed and it's in a wealthy neighbourhood. We thought we might be able to find a spot nearby to get a view of Popocatepetl. So we walked up a hill past magnificent villas and luxurious haciendas and all of a sudden, it was as though we'd stepped over an invisible borderline. We found ourselves surrounded by shacks nailed together from old crates and sheet metal. The paving came to an abrupt end and the streets were a sea of mud with lots of children wading in it. Some of them shouted at us and begged for money; an adolescent mestiza invited us into a shack that didn't even have a door. Then a little girl in tattered rags ran up to us. She was barely four, and she held out a wilted flower, a chrysanthemum or something, and tried to sell it to us. That's when I thought that no matter where you are, you get tangled up in some kind of spider's web that you can't get free of.'

'Wait a minute, look at this,' she said, interrupting him.

They were now broadcasting a clip of the student demonstration that had started the whole thing. It showed the moments before the police attacked: a phalanx of men in uniforms with plastic shields protecting their faces, a crowd of students singing the national anthem, girls sticking flowers in the policemen's shields. There was no movement, each side waiting for the other to advance, young men and women sitting on the ground with burning candles set on the paving-stones in front of them, chanting: Our hands are empty! Then the phalanx of policemen began to shuffle forward. The first frenzied punches. Screams of pain, and then the noise of crunching blows, angry shouts, the pounding of boots on the pavement, the cries of the beaten.

Alice sobbed. There was absolute silence. Everyone was looking at the screen. Once it was over, Alice wiped her eyes. 'That was awful,' she said quietly, 'But the fact that you broadcast it, that's . . . it's the beginning of freedom.' She embraced him. For a moment all he could see was the dark blue of her eyes, which were again full of tears.

Back at television headquarters he went straight into the garage, where a very emotional meeting was just winding up. They were discussing, as they had been constantly over the past few days, whether future demonstrations should be broadcast live. The management were still refusing to allow this. Most of the technical staff, as Little Ivens told him when he sat down beside him, were making live broadcasts an unconditional demand, otherwise they were prepared to go on strike. 'Are you going to get up and say something?'

'I don't know what's already been said.'

'It's obvious we should do it live. After all, we broadcast every stupid hockey game live,' said Little Ivens.

Pavel nodded. He listened for a while to the passionate speeches, speeches that he would have found entirely persuasive and reasonable were they not being delivered by the very same people who, only a few days before, had been willing to say the exact opposite. During the day, when he had been running from faculty to faculty and freezing on the square, the course of events had apparently shifted so radically that the trend now seemed almost irreversible. That was why everyone was scurrying over to the side of the victors before it was too late.

But who would testify on their behalf should they all be considered the losers?

We have no witnesses, we have no one to appeal to and our work will be used against us.

He dialled a familiar number. 'Is that you, Ali? You're not asleep yet?'

'No, not yet. I'm reading. I don't even know what time it is. Has something happened?'

'No, nothing. It's just that I can't get to sleep.'

'I'm glad you called.'

'I've been lying here for an hour staring at the ceiling. I see beetles swarming about up there. They're having races. I'm watching them and betting on this angry beetle who's losing and biting the leg of the one in front of him. Then I realized they're not beetles, they're people. I can even recognize their faces.'

'Darling, is something wrong?'

'No, nothing, it's just those beetles. They're closing in on me.'

'Have you been drinking?'

'It's beetles I'm seeing, not white mice.'

'Should I come over?'

'It's too late.'

'But I'm used to that. You know I'm used to night shifts.'

'That's different. But I'd like to see you. I'll drive over and pick you up. At least you'll see I haven't been drinking.'

'You don't have to come for me. I'll take a taxi.'

She was there in half an hour. She kissed him standing in the doorway. 'Aren't you feeling well?'

'Why do you think that?'

'I can tell.'

'I'm a lot better now. I suddenly felt I couldn't breathe, but it was just a brief sensation.'

'Should I call a doctor?'

'I can't stand doctors. Only someone afraid to take his own life will put himself in the hands of doctors.'

'Then you should lie down at least.' She made him swallow a pill, then put a cold compress on the left side of his chest.

'The work's been piling up on me,' he said. 'I have to finish everything before I go, and there's so little time left.'

'Don't talk to me about your work, or about going!' She put her hand on his forehead. Her hand was soft and warm and smelt of leaves.

'When I come back, we'll get married,' he said.

'I know. But we don't have to get married. It's not important.'

'Fine. Come and lie down with me.'

'I'd rather sit beside you.'

'Lie down with me. I want you to be as close to me as possible.'

'You want me as close as possible, and yet you're going away to the other side of the world.'

He watched her undress. 'I'll only be gone a month, but if you don't want me to go, I won't.'

'No, I don't want anything of the kind. I just feel anxious. But it's no big deal. It's my condition.'

'There's nothing to be afraid of. I'll come back whenever you want.'

'It's not you who decides when you come back. You

141

can't just go and leave the rest of them there.'

'I've always made my own decisions.'

'Don't be so arrogant. No one ever makes decisions about himself alone.'

'So who makes them, then?'

'God, or the angels.'

His boss, Halama, was warning them not to get caught up in the mood of the crowds. Of course, we're all trying to improve living and working conditions and achieve greater freedom, but at this moment in time the very foundations of our system are in danger—everything that generations have worked for, that people have not hesitated to give their lives for.

His speeches were usually lacklustre and soporific; now his words were charged with emotion. If we continue to submit to the demands of the mob, soon no one will be able to stop the forces that have unleashed this whole campaign. They will sweep away the government, they will sweep away us, they will sweep away our whole system, they will set us back a century. Therefore, we must calm people down, not add petrol to the flames. It was a serious error to broadcast shots of the police action. Police intervene like that everywhere in the world.

Someone in the room shouted that everywhere else in the world, they show it the same day on television.

'Yes, they do,' admitted the boss, 'but everywhere else the viewers are more hardened. They're used to that sort of thing.'

Someone in the room began to whistle. Others joined in.

They oughtn't to whistle too loudly, Pavel thought. Halama's prediction was, after all, correct from his own point of view. He feared for the system that had enabled him to be boss, that had enabled them all to work where they were working. If that system collapsed, the television announcers and everyone who stood behind them would be the first to go. He remembered Alice, weeping over what they had broadcast. The beginning of freedom, she had said. But would any of them survive the kind of freedom that was in the air, the kind that he was trying to support? Fortunately he was too tired to wonder whether he was building a cathedral of freedom, or merely digging his own grave. He tried to slip out of the room, but Sokol caught up with him in the hall and told him that the student strike committee was still in session and that they should go there now.

'They'll be in session again tomorrow.'

'Tomorrow might be too late. Don't forget, everything's at stake now.'

He'd already heard that once today. And after all, he'd always longed to film freely what he saw, or rather, what was hidden behind what he saw. Why should he squander this opportunity now, when he might not have it much longer?

The drama faculty was housed in a street that bore the name of an old emperor who had left his mark on the city in the past—everything had been at stake then, too. Two students, acting as guards, were walking up and down in front of the building, and they had to wait until they let them go inside. Then they had to wait again until someone from the committee could give them an interview. Meanwhile the students brought them coffee and a tray full of sandwiches. Although it was late in the evening, the lights were still on in all the rooms. Young people were running busily up and down the corridors, computer terminals glowed in one of the lecture halls, and in another female students bent over large sheets of paper, making posters. As soon as the paint on the posters was dry, others would roll them up and take them away. Most of the benches had been removed from the large lecture hall, and a young man with glasses, whose face seemed familiar, probably from one of the demonstrations, was speaking. Students who were interested were sitting in a circle around him, while others had already crawled into sleeping-bags lining the wall at the far end of the room.

Several years ago, Pavel had been invited here to take part in a panel discussion. He had tried to explain, as best he could, not only the technique but also the philosophy behind his work. In the rat race of the present, when people no longer have time to look around them, we have to show them what they miss every day. This means not always cutting rapidly from image to image, but lingering on things that might seem ordinary to us. Music videos, for example, are expressions of the neurosis that is engulfing us.

They had heard him out and then argued with him. They felt he was attacking music videos because they came from the world beyond the barbed wire. He had felt a veiled hostility in their responses: hostility towards himself and, even more, towards the world they believed he represented.

At last a pale and weary young man appeared, the one they were to interview. Pavel shot a close-up of his face, his moving lips, his reddish eyes. The words the young man spoke were no more than a distant drone. He talked about non-violence, about moral renewal, about the freedom to believe in anything you wanted to believe in, about how they had to grasp the historical opportunity that had just presented itself.

What was an historical opportunity?

Merely a moment when people believed they had managed to disrupt the flow of history and thus open up room for manoeuvre. Whether they had actually done so, or whether they had actually closed something off is a judgement that could only be passed by history itself.

The interview was over. The young man had to hurry back to his committee meeting. If they would like to wait, he said, the meeting would be over in about an hour. Then they would learn more.

Sokol looked uncertainly at his cameraman.

'Sure, we can stay here until morning, if you think it's useful. It's certainly more interesting here than at home in bed.'

He went back into the main lecture hall where the bespectacled young man was still talking. Meanwhile the number of sleepers on the floor had increased. He found a free spot by the wall, folded his coat to serve as a pillow and got ready to stretch out. A student who was lying to his left watched him. 'If you haven't got a blanket, go into number eight. They'll give you something there.' Her clear articulation and her resonant voice suggested that she was an aspiring actress.

'Thanks,' he said, 'but I won't be here long so it's hardly worth it.'

'Then you can have one of mine. I've got two.'

'Thank you, but I really don't need it. I'm warm enough.' She could have been his daughter. Everyone here could have been his child. What would his son have been doing now?

'Suit yourself,' said the girl, and she turned over to go back to sleep. An annoying light filled the room, and the air was acrid with the smell of tired human bodies. For a moment it reminded him of nights in his prison cell long ago, except for the girl beside him. And that strange, almost exultant mood that seemed to bring everyone, including him, closer together. This feeling of solidarity had surprised him. He wasn't prepared for it, and in fact he'd always resisted it—or certainly ever since he'd become aware of the laws that governed life in the prison.

Perhaps if he hadn't gone to prison he might have married and would now have children of his own. Not only did prison teach him that he always had to watch what he said and did in front of other people, but he was out of circulation at a time when his contemporaries were forming relationships, and he squandered the rest of that time when they released him. He'd been driven by a mixture of ambition, anger and guilt about his mother. He'd also been poor. He had wanted to go to university, but his prison record meant that was out of the question. He'd worked as a driver's mate and later got a job in a photography lab, and then was finally accepted on to a correspondence course. During that time, he'd met a lot of women and had made love to some of them, though he'd trusted no one. He hadn't wanted to start a family with any of them, and anyway, most of them already had children. In the end he lost the ability to tell whether he was genuinely fond of a woman he'd met or not. And his son remained unborn.

The door to the lecture hall kept opening and closing, and the sound of many voices mingled and overlapped. A telephone was constantly ringing on the other side of the wall, pulling him back from the brink of sleep.

The day before he flew off to Mexico, he went to his

studio with Albina. It was still afternoon, but they took their clothes off and lay on the couch and made love. Then they drank wine and coffee, made love again, drank more coffee, and she told his fortune from the grounds. She saw precipices and abysses that seemed impossible to scale or cross, and it made her sad. Fortunately, above that she thought she recognized a bird of prey with its wings spread wide. That might be him, and he might fly across the mountains and further still, but would he come back to her? Then she remembered that he had once mentioned a story he was working on and would like to film one day. She asked him to tell it to her.

It was just a rough idea, he said.

'I'd still like to hear it. As a way of saying goodbye.'

'It's not a story to say goodbye with.'

'Why not?'

'It's about something else.' He put his arms around her. 'I don't remember ever mentioning it to you.'

'I'd like to hear it.'

'In fact, it's not really a story, it's just a bunch of images. I enjoy coming up with images. Maybe one day I'll string them together into a story, and that will be for you.'

'So, come on, tell me. Don't make me twist your arm.' She was lying beside him and he could caress her body, touch her breasts, as he spoke. 'Who's the story about?'

'You know, I don't even have a name for him. He's just called 'he'. Sometimes I think that he's really me, but then we split again, because I'm different. I'm sorry, I'm not being very clear. This person is a carpenter like my father. But that's not important. He's successful and rich and famous for his carvings. Then he has a bad accident and loses his right hand.'

'How old is he when this happens?'

'Not very old, but by that time he was already famous. He doesn't want this to stop him working, so he tries to carve with his left hand, but when he does manage to finish something, it's as though it had been made by someone else. That crushes him. He feels as though he's lost himself.'

'Doesn't he have a family?'

'He has two sons, but they don't live with him. Their

mother took them away when they were still small. After
the accident, they come to see him in his studio where he
has a lot of carvings, some finished, some not. There's a
bird taking flight, a tiger getting ready to jump. Icarus, and
Prometheus bound. His sons want to know what he's
going to do now. He replies that they needn't worry, he's
already done enough in this life and that he is simply
going to live and think.

'He really tries. He walks about the city and the coun-
tryside beyond, but the things he sees demand that he give
them a shape, and he has to reply that he can't, and that
depresses him.

'He stops going out of doors. He drives things and
people out of his mind, until he finds himself in a state of
emptiness, one that bears no resemblance to any coun-
tryside or any space. It is true emptiness.'

'And what about God?'

'He doesn't believe in God.'

'But God exists.'

'No one knows that. But he's not waiting for God. If
he's waiting for anything, it's for death, and he's curious
about what the face of death will look like. Will it be like
an old woman who creeps about the world with a scythe,
or will it be a beautiful young girl who approaches him
with open arms?

'One day he gets an invitation to visit an old uncle of
his whom everyone in the family thinks is crazy. He has
nothing better to do, so he accepts the invitation. After all,
he's living in emptiness. I imagine the emptiness of this
particular day as a yellowish fog through which the occa-
sional outline of a house becomes visible. Suddenly,
however, a black raven emerges out of this yellow fog. It
stands on the rim of a fountain and stares at him. Then it
spreads its wings as if it were getting ready to fly away, but
it doesn't. It merely watches him through its small, clever
eyes as he enters his uncle's block.

'The uncle has an interesting face that reminds him a
little of Spencer Tracy. The one thing that gives the uncle's
life meaning is drawing up family trees. He looks for direct
ancestors and, as far as his strength will permit, searches

through other branches of the family as well. The uncle tells him that he's managed to get as far back as the six- teenth century and has found unknown soldiers, surgeons, impoverished gentry, martyrs tortured by the Inquisition, village magistrates and many generations of serfs. He has discovered a branch that once lived in Burgundy. In his cupboard there are piles of maps and reams of graph paper on which he had drawn the different branches of his genealogical charts. The uncle announces that he intends to leave all this to him.

'He objects that he's never been interested in such things. The uncle, however, brings out a box full of docu- ments: among them are the originals of birth certificates, purchase agreements, faded letters, ribbons, dried flowers, funeral notices, copies of parish registers. The meaning of my work, he says, was to know where I came from and therefore where I'm going.

'What can a few dates and names of long-dead people possibly tell you?' he asks his uncle. His uncle leans close to him and whispers, "They speak to me. They're not dead, they just move in a different space."

'The following week he hires a taxi to take all the docu- ments away. When they are carrying out the last carton and he's getting ready to pay the driver, he notices an enormous raven perched on a pile of dirt and paving- stones, ob- serving him. He understands that he is being given a sign but he doesn't understand what it means. Am I boring you?'

'How could you possibly bore me?'

'In any case, it was you who led me to do this story.'

'Me?'

'By being the way you are.'

'What is the way I am?'

'Mysterious.'

She kissed him.

'It's only after the uncle dies that he starts work. He finds his uncle's final piece of paper, the one that brings him closest to some kind of beginning, although twelve generations means nothing in the history of any family. On the tip of the tree is the name Agrippa Sever, born on the fourth of November in the hamlet of Chiliene, in the region of Ellis. He copies this information down. He doesn't know what country to look for the region of Ellis in, but he can imagine the era. A Gothic castle perched on an inaccessible rocky promontory, a stony road along which a pair of oxen are pulling a heavy wagon.

'The hamlet of Chiliene, as he discovers by checking old maps, is now called Kyllene, and is situated on a north-western promontory of the Peloponnese. He will have to go there if he wants to continue his investigation. When he arrives, he tries to make enquiries at the parish church but he draws a blank. The priest no longer has the register from that period. He takes him out to the cemetery, but he can't find a single grave older than one hundred and fifty years, not a single headstone that suggests the name he is looking for. The priest sends him to the district town on the edge of the sea.'

'You've seen it?'

'Perhaps, in a movie. Or I dreamt about it. Stone buildings, cobbled streets, everything white, pink oleander blooming in the gardens, figs and olives ripening. Dark-skinned, black-haired children are playing in the narrow streets. A donkey is pulling a two-wheeled cart to the top of a hill.

'He asks about the archives, but no one understands him. They take him into a bar where several sailors and some young women are sitting. They offer him wine. Then he's astonished to see the carving of a raven sitting on a ledge beside the door. He realizes his trip will not be in vain. And sure enough, the next day in the archives, he finds the name he's been looking for. He also discovers that the grandfather of this man came here with the army of the Venetian doge.'

'So he has to go to Italy?'

'Yes. Suddenly, he gets the fever. He aches to discover more ancestors. The Italian soldier's name was Severus. What if this man was related to the dynasty of Roman emperors? The idea obsesses him. Not so much because he longs to be the descendant of a line of unremarkable emperors, but he sees something that he can hold on to. But how is he to bridge a gap of thousands of years? Back to a time when barbarians were rampaging through Europe, devastating towns and countries, when even kings and princes seemed to emerge from darkness, and their descendants seemed to vanish into it once more?

'He continues his journey backwards in time, though it becomes more and more difficult. He chats up unknown archivists. He talks his way into monasteries, rectories, libraries. He writes letters. Some of his correspondents treat him as an eccentric; others think that they might be able to get something out of him, if not money then at least something valuable.

'The sons visit him again. They find that his studio is now empty. Only a few blocks of unworked wood remain, and the carving of a bird with its wings outstretched. They try to persuade their father to give up. They shout at him: you've gone mad, you should get help. He throws them out.

'He probably should seek a doctor's help, but instead he continues his search. In his life now there passes a procession of landscapes, cities, rectories, monasteries. Almost illegible documents flash before his eyes. The letters seem to dance and recompose themselves into words and names. Other landscapes and other people enter his life, people long since lost, of whom only a name remained, yet he sees them. Once, he sees them as if in a wedding procession, dressed in ancient costumes, walking to the sounds of Gregorian chant to a small church set on a white rock. At other times he sees his ancestors in a band of warriors filing along a jungle path and dancing half-naked around fires. He hears the hunters cheer when they strike down their prey. The images increase. At first they come to him only at night, then they begin appearing by day as well. He looks at the sea and suddenly sees a line of warships—triremes—nearing the shore. Or, from the window of an inn, he catches a glimpse of twelve lictors in togas. Once he notices that he is being watched from a distance by a hairy man with a low, sloping, simian forehead. The man is gripping a club in his enormous right hand. He stops to allow the man to catch up with him, but he merely circles around him, as though skirting a circle whose perimeter he cannot enter. This happens several days in a row, until one night the man finally appears by his bedside. He asks the man what he wants, but he knows the man will not reply: he is from a different space, and is of a different essence. He is merely a shadow of someone more ancient from whom he is descended.

'Then the shadows visit him more frequently. They come to him in his studio. They sit around in corners, or at night they stand around his bed and sometimes he can hear them whispering among themselves. Sometimes he can understand fragments of sentences, and he jumps out of bed and, with his left hand, scribbles down what they are apparently trying to tell him: If I have at last found mercy before thy face . . . nearer to thee, our Lord, nearer to the fire . . . clay from clay, ashes from ashes, dust from dust, life from death . . . O, bow down to the powerful and lead our souls into . . . Sometimes he even tries to sketch the faces. The wild, hairy faces of the men and the bare faces of the women. Their low foreheads, flattened noses and tiny chins give them a savage, almost animal look. Their names too begin to sound stranger and stranger. They are short and often remind him of the cry of birds, the sounds of animals or the howling of the wind. He learns that SiSiSi was the friend of Tektek, but when, for how long and where he lived, he cannot discover. He tries to summon him forth again, but none of the shadows ever returns, as though they have to make room for others. They begin to behave with more and more abandon, their sentences become less coherent, then they utter single words, then stuttering syllables, and finally they seem to interpolate animal yelps among the syllables. The savage howling of ancient beasts of prey, the deep throaty roar of bears and, almost constantly now, the hiss of approaching snakes and the slurping yawn of mussels and clams. It's exhausting. He still tries to sketch the outlines of these shadows but he can no longer perceive their shapes. Perhaps they no longer have a shape, perhaps their shapes are decayed by time; he can only see coloured, blurred spots that fly and circle around him.

'Then his strength runs out. He no longer gets out of bed. He only looks on as the luminous half-forms dance, and listens to the noises that draw together and blend until they sound like rushing water. He feels that he's no longer lying down, but falling. He falls into depths that are more bottomless than the sky, and as he falls the light around him becomes calm and clear, the sounds blend into a single tone, a penetrating whistle, which permeates him so that he no longer knows whether it's coming from outside or from within. At that moment he understands that he is perceiving the divine presence, the presence of God, and he whispers, *God*: his last word.

'They find him in the middle of the empty studio, lying among scraps of paper covered with words in an incomprehensible language and sketches of improbable creatures. The dead man is smiling. One of those who find him says, "The poor bugger must have gone off his rocker."'

The room is silent, like the dead man's studio. Perhaps she had fallen asleep, but her eyes were staring wide into the darkness outside the window. 'And the bird. What about the raven?' she asked finally.

'I forgot about him.' Her question disappointed him. 'He discovers that one of his ancestors had the nickname Corvus.'

'That's a strange story. It's not the kind of story I'd expect from you. It's as though someone else had invented it, someone else inside you, someone who longs to have faith in something.' She leaned over to him and began to kiss him, her cheeks damp with tears. He didn't know if she was crying because the story moved her, or because she was sorry for him, or because they were about to part.

What was faith?

Faith was a longing that pretended to be a conviction.

The noise in the room suddenly stopped. Then a powerful male voice announced that they needed five messengers to go out into the countryside that very night. They would need to be prepared for any eventuality because the situation in the countryside was unclear, and they had unconfirmed reports that armed militia units were standing by at the outskirts of the city, ready to intervene. The voice listed all the places the messengers were to go, the most distant of which was at the far end of the country. Volunteers immediately stood up.

At that moment he heard Sokol's voice offering them the use of the television van.

So he got up. It seemed unlikely that there would be any shooting, but if so, and he and his camera were to survive, he would get some unique footage, though of course there always was shooting somewhere in the world, and that kind of unique footage always looked the same.

A long-haired boy and a girl whose face was still that of a child got into the van. Other students brought a bundle of posters and some flyers.

As they left he looked out of the window and saw several hands waving at them. It was the first time strangers had ever waved to a car in which he was sitting. Both the kids were sitting beside him talking quietly about people he didn't know. The girl addressed the boy as Dan, and the boy called her Dora.

It was already past midnight, and the streets were completely empty. There was no sign of militia units.

He pulled out a packet of cigarettes and offered them to the students beside him. The young man refused; the girl accepted and he lit it for her. She noticed that his lighter was shaped like a tiny revolver. 'It's a good thing we're armed,' she remarked.

'We don't shoot in this country,' said the boy—as though he could remember. 'When the shooting starts, someone has to come from somewhere else to deal with it.'

'You can kill without shooting,' countered the girl.

'Have they killed anyone you know?' he asked her.

'No one I know,' she replied, 'but that's not important. You can poison people so slowly that no one notices.'

'Do you mean with television?'

'That's possible,' she said, 'but there are lots of ways of doing it. Like the way they poisoned us at school for fifteen years.'

'Are you counting nursery school?'

'That's where it starts.' She laughed. 'But now it's all over.'

Sokol, who was sitting beside the driver, turned to her. 'Too bad you didn't say that on camera.'

'Anyone will tell you that any time,' she said. 'Too bad it took you so long to come to us.'

'We would have come sooner, but they wouldn't have broadcast our footage. And maybe you wouldn't have spoken this way either.'

'Perhaps,' admitted the student. 'Everything in its own good time.'

The van drove out of the city, but they had to go slowly because the road was veiled in mist. The girl leaned her head on the boy's shoulder and closed her eyes.

'What are you studying?' Pavel asked the young man.

'As a matter of fact, just what you're doing. I mean I'm studying to be a cameraman.'

'That's good. You can take over from me, if necessary.'

'Why not?' he said. 'It would be more interesting.'

'What do you mean?'

'I couldn't stand your programmes, any of them. Whenever they turned the television on at home, I'd leave the room. Now here I am, riding in the same car as you.'

'Maybe we found it even more disgusting than you did,' said Sokol. 'We had even more reason to.'

'But you did it,' objected the student. 'Even so, you did it.'

'You went on studying too,' said Sokol, 'even though you knew they were poisoning you.'

'That's an interesting comparison. But it's not quite the same thing.'

'Maybe you'll be able to do everything better now, when you take over from us,' Pavel interjected.

'I hope so, otherwise I wouldn't want to touch it.'

That's what you say now, Pavel thought, when you have a hope that things will change. But he said nothing. He lit another cigarette and looked out into the impenetrable fog.

He too hoped that things would change. People like this student would come to replace him because he was one of the poisoners. And he would acquiesce because in the end, he too wanted everything to be done better. So this was what the beginning of freedom was like. If it would not be for him, then at least it would be for his unborn son.

2

THE CAMERAS WERE set up, the writing-desk lit. The old man held in his hand some sheets of paper from which to read. He seemed gaunt, tired and old. Nevertheless, his voice was as harsh and domineering as ever. 'Can we begin?' He clearly wanted to get this over with. A resignation forced upon him by popular demonstrations in the streets, by a people who now eagerly awaited his final humiliation.

'Two more minutes, Mr President.' Pavel also wanted to get it over with, even though no one would see him doing it. He had not wanted to see this man at close range again, though it would probably be for the last time. 'Who else but you?' they had said.

'Stand by, Mr President!'

The old man sat down, pulled out a handkerchief and blew his nose. He was obviously feeling very emotional. When they had elected him head of state years ago, he had been moved to tears. Many others across the country had no doubt wept too, from despair or shame. But most had looked on, as Pavel had, with merely curious or shocked indifference.

'Fifteen seconds! I'll give you the signal with my hand, Mr President.'

The paper, covered with words that had been enlarged several times so the half-blind man could read them, trembled. Pavel gave him the signal, and the old man began to deliver the last speech he would ever make before falling into the dark hole of utter forgetting.

Through the viewfinder, he saw the face he had filmed so often; the microphones captured the voice they had captured so many times before. The voice quavered, and the face looked even more gloomy and serious than usual. It seemed that not only had he written this speech himself, he had also invested it with some real feeling, and now was now trying to speak from the heart, to reach the people to whom he had so often delivered vacuous appeals, messages in which emptiness was wrapped up in grandiloquent nothingness.

This time he spoke with dry matter-of-factness. The people were calling for a new government and for the president's resignation, he said. He had received many letters on these matters, some supporting him, some critical. He thanked everyone for their views, positive or negative, for at least now he knew what people really thought. He had decided to appoint a new government and then resign.

'Ever since my youth, I have believed in the same bright ideals, and I continue to believe in them to this day.' He was speaking of his illusory faith from a dark hole, a drowning raven whose broken wings beat against the stormy waves that had finally engulfed him. 'There were certainly errors, but those errors were in people, not in the ideal, and therefore, I will remain faithful to the ideal as, I believe, will most of us.'

Pavel watched the morose face in his viewfinder with purely professional attention. He felt no emotion, not the slightest hint of compassion for the old man. He observed him as he would observe a slithering snake, an eviscerated rat or a warehouse full of toxic waste.

What would have happened had this ruler not emerged from the darkness into which he was now returning? Had he not appeared and defiled Pavel's life, defiled the life of everyone in this country? Would his life have been less tarnished? Would he now be standing on the brink of a dark hole that was about to swallow him up?

For the last time, the president wished everybody success in overcoming the present difficulties, and a quiet Christmas and a happy New Year.

His son would not have been born anyway.

The speech was over. The lighting technicians switched off the lights, the sound men put away the microphones.

The old man stepped up to him. He seemed to hesitate, as though he were afraid of being rebuffed, then he offered his hand and thanked him. Pavel returned the thanks and wished him well.

Who would take his place? And who would film the new president's speeches?

His mother was in hospital now. She had been careless about heating up some tea on the gas stove, and her dressing-gown had caught fire. Surprisingly, she had managed to tear it off, but not before the flames had seared her left arm and hip.

'For a young person, this would be no more than a painful but minor setback,' a female doctor had told him. 'But at her age the skin sometimes refuses to heal.'

'I understand.' He was holding a bouquet that he had bought for his mother. It occurred to him that his mother wouldn't notice the flowers anyway, so he could give them to the doctor. But the right moment had passed, and besides, it was probably inappropriate to pay the doctor off with a handful of flowers.

'If you need medicine, or any other sort of help . . .'

'Please, don't worry. We will do everything we can,' the doctor reassured him.

If he'd had a home of his own where his mother could have lived with him, this would probably not have happened. But the truth was, she was the reason he had not married. He could have spent far more time with her than he had, but he found her mental confusion repugnant. When he was with her, he thought mostly about how to get away again as quickly as possible.

She lay in a small room with three other women, her bandaged arm resting on the white counterpane, her eyes closed. The air in the room was overheated and stale, and he could smell the elderly bodies and some kind of disinfectant.

'The old lady sleeps a lot,' said the woman in the next bed. 'She moaned the whole of the first night, but it's better now.' The woman was young, and her face was apparently permanently scarred by burns.

He ran some water into a lemonade bottle and put the flowers into it, then sat down in a chair beside his mother's bed. 'Mother?'

Slowly she opened her eyes and looked at him. Her expression was blank.

'It's me, Mother.'

'Who's me?'

'Pavel.'

'It's your son,' said the neighbour. 'You told me about him yourself.'

'Is it you?'

'It's me.'

'It's good of you to come. Where am I? This isn't my bed.'

'You're in hospital, Mother.'

'How did you find me here?'

'He looked for you, didn't he,' said the neighbour. 'He knows his mother's here.'

'Yes, he says I used to be his mother,' she allowed. 'Isn't Daddy coming?'

'No.'

'He probably hasn't got the time,' said the neighbour. 'It's like I said, no one's got the time any more. My husband hasn't been to see me for a week. He just phones. They say the president resigned. Is that true?' she asked Pavel.

He nodded.

'What a pity,' said the neighbour. 'A pity I have to be here, I mean. If I were at home, we'd celebrate.'

'But he's resigned so often already,' said his mother.

'Not this one,' laughed the neighbour.

'It doesn't matter,' said the mother. 'They all have to go one day. Have they put him in a hospital too?'

'Who?'

'The one you're always talking about.'

'No,' he said. 'Do you feel any pain?'

'How could I feel any pain? They've taken away my body.'

He stroked her hand. He couldn't think what to say to her. Perhaps she would die in a few days. He should do something for her. What can you do for a mother whose body is departing and whose soul is already gone? Talk to her about hope. But what kind of hope would she understand? And what kind of hope did she have left? What kind of hope did he believe in himself? What would he want in her situation?

He'd want not to be among complete strangers. He'd want someone to hold his hand. Once again he stroked her unbandaged hand. It was cold, wrinkled and rough.

'The air in here is strange,' she said. 'I don't think I'm at home. And I don't know where little Pavel is.'

'I'm Pavel.'

'You're just making fun of me. Little Pavel was my son. A tiny little boy.'

'Well, who do you think I am? It's just that I've grown up since then.'

'Little Pavel never grew up. I don't know what became of him. He was a good boy. I was fond of him, and he was fond of me.' She sobbed under her breath. 'It makes me sad that I haven't seen him so long.' She closed her eyes and continued to sob.

The telephone rang. '*El Señor* Fuka?'

'*Al aparato.*' He wasn't properly awake and didn't know what time it was, but it was still deep night outside his window. The fan on the ceiling was turning noisily. He was lying in his hotel room. Karel Sokol was sleeping soundly in the other bed. They'd drunk too many tequilas last night. Why hadn't Sokol answered the telephone? But no, the call was apparently for Pavel. '*Quien habla?*'

'*Un momento. Le llaman.*'

'Dr Valentová here. Can you hear me?'

'Yes, I can hear you very clearly, Dr Valentová.'

'I'm Albina's mother.'

'Yes, I know that, doctor.'

'I just wanted to tell you the news. I took my daughter to the hospital last night.'

'Oh, God! Has anything serious happened?'

'She began to bleed, but there's still hope. I just thought you should know.'

'Yes, thank you. But I don't know . . . Do you think I should come home?'

'I have no idea what your responsibilities are. But my daughter isn't in the best of shape, psychologically. I mean, you know what this child would mean to her . . . '

'I do. Please tell her I'll come. Tell her I'll come on the first available flight.'

'I'll give you her number at the hospital. Perhaps you should tell her yourself.'

'Yes. Thank you. I'll call her.'

Four o'clock in the morning, which means it's ten in the morning at home, no, eleven.

Still half asleep, Sokol asked, 'Is something wrong?'

'I'm going to have to go back.'

'Back where?'

'Back home.'

'What—are you crazy? Was that production calling? They agreed that we could extend our stay.'

'It wasn't production. You can go back to sleep.'

'How can I sleep when you've just gone off your rocker?'

'I'll explain in the morning.'

He should call the hospital right away but he didn't have anything definite to tell her. Besides, he was confused. The first thing he had to do was reserve a flight. Before that he had to sort things out with Sokol. He couldn't just get up and fly away when the work was barely half finished. So the first thing he had to do was call the hospital and find out if it still made any sense to fly back now. But before that he had to know something definite. And the day after tomorrow they were supposed to fly to Merida, and he couldn't get out of that because the shooting had all been arranged . . .

When morning came everything seemed far less urgent than it had in the dead of night. The telephone conversation had become an unreal nightmare.

'Too bad you never introduced me to her,' said Sokol. 'I'd like to see the woman you're willing to drop everything for. You can't help her anyway,' he went on. 'Her mother's a doctor. She'll look after her. You've got responsibilities here. You can't just pack up and leave. She has to understand that.'

It sounded convincing. Besides, he would probably never get to this part of the world again, and there was still so much he wanted to see and film.

The next morning he called the hospital from the airport. He left a message for Albina saying he would return as soon as he could. He flew off to Merida, but he was now in a rush. In a single day, he tried to accomplish what they had to do in a week. Then the Indian chauffeur that they had hired gently remonstrated with him. Why were these white men always in such a hurry? If you are in too much of a hurry, he explained, your spirit won't be able to keep up with you. If you don't wait for it, it will never catch up.

His mother opened her eyes again. 'Where am I, anyway?'

'You were asleep,' he said. 'You were lucky not to be burnt to death.'

His mother laughed. 'I was lucky. I used to be lucky, once. And what are you doing, Pavel? Are you lucky too?'

'We're all lucky now, Mrs Fuková,' interrupted the neighbour. 'We're all ecstatic.'

'Yes,' said his mother. 'We're delighted you came, Pavel, that you're here with me, that you'll stay with me.'

His mother closed her eyes again. He ought to stay here with her, not rush away. He ought to stay here with her till the very end.

3

HE FINISHED WORK in the editing room earlier then he expected, and an empty stretch of time loomed before him. He saw a small group of strangers in the corridor, conversing with great animation. The building was now full of unfamiliar faces, some of whom might have been returning after years of absence—not to this building, which was practically new, but to jobs they had once held. These people made him uneasy. He walked by them as quickly as he could. The porter in the lodge acknowledged him with a nod on his way out. At least they hadn't replaced him. Not yet.

It was a cold evening outside. The paving-stones were greasy with layers of soot, dust and mist, and the air was acrid with smoke. He got into his sports car and drove the short distance to the city centre. He realized he was close to the store where Eva worked, and could drop in. He hadn't seen her for several days. Somehow, there never seemed to be enough time.

With Sokol, he had driven around the towns and the cities, mostly in the north of the country. Out of the fog that shrouded the countryside, softening the outlines of people and things, demonstrators emerged, flags waved and speakers rose spontaneously to address spontaneous gatherings. Mostly they were people who had not been allowed to speak for years. They clambered on to piles of rock, balanced on the rims of fountains and on pedestals of statues whose removal they demanded, just as they demanded the removal of those who had bowed down before these statues. They spun visions of how everyone's life, including Pavel's own, would quickly be transformed and rise above the poverty in which it had for so long been mired. Others, who preferred actions to words, climbed on to rooftops to remove the snow-covered symbols of yesterday's power. They pulled down street signs and fastened in their place new plaques scrawled with names that until recently had been unmentionable, and they sometimes gathered threateningly under the windows of abandoned Party secretariats, ready to break in and begin, or rather complete, the purging. In every face he saw a kind of ecstasy that looked almost sexual.

When he had last seen Eva, he had noticed this same look on her face. In strangers, it seemed to make their faces more attractive, or at least more interesting, but Eva's ecstasy had repelled him. What was she hoping for, what did she expect the altered circumstances would bring her, and him? What could she possibly understand of these events? Perhaps he was simply repelled by an emotion in her which was not occasioned by him.

He parked in a side-street right in front of the entrance to a bar.

It was packed inside, as it always was in all the bars at that time of day. He stood by the taps and ordered a large vodka. On the wall, along with posters of half-naked models and advertisements for beer, was a picture of the new president. An American pop song playing softly from a set of speakers was drowned out in the din of voices. A massive man standing beside him was trying to communicate his opinion of the situation to the barman. 'We're being far too soft on them. It's going to backfire.'

'Their turn will come,' said the barman. 'Everything takes time.'

'The way I see it, either we beat the shit out of them or

they're going to beat the shit out of us again tomorrow. It's like rats. They leave sinking ships, and if you don't beat them to death they'll just crawl on board another ship and go on eating everything in sight.'

Where do I belong? he thought. With those who'll do the beating or with those who'll get beaten to death? He didn't know anybody here, but he wondered if someone might recognize him. His picture sometimes appeared in the television guide. He felt uneasy. He ordered another vodka, tossed it back and left the bar.

Eva was rearranging something on a shelf when he walked in. She turned around as soon as she heard the door creak. 'So it's you? What are you doing here?'

'I just got back to town and I've come straight to see you.'

'That's nice of you. I'm closing up soon. Will you come home with me tonight?'

'Where else would I go?'

'I don't know. I don't know where you go when you're not with me.'

'You can close up right away,' he said. 'People have other things to think about now, besides buying hand-kerchiefs or socks.'

'Business is always slack after Christmas.' She got up, went to the door, locked it and hung up a sign that said: GONE TO THE POST OFFICE. 'I'm here on my own today. I still have some accounts to do, and then I should take the money to the post office. You can wait in the back and I'll make you some coffee.'

The room behind the shop was partly like an office and partly reminiscent of a women's powder-room, with a basin, a mirror, a shelf crammed with little bottles and vials and creams, a table and two armchairs, one of which un-folded into a bed. On top of a metal filing cabinet stood a hotplate with a kettle on it in which water was apparently always on the boil. The room was hot. He took off his sweater, sat down on the chair and lit a cigarette. She made coffee for him and for herself, then sat down opposite him. She had spent all day in the shop, yet her hair and make-up were flawless, and her white blouse seemed so clean it might have come straight off a hanger.

'So, what was it like out there?'

He said that he'd had a lot of work. Everything was in flux now, so much was happening, there was lots to see and therefore lots to film, and no one had to approve what he shot any more.

She asked how his mother was, but he hadn't had a chance to go to the hospital that day. Over the phone they told him that the burns were healing surprisingly well. It was his mother's mind that was beyond healing.

'What's Robin been up to?' he asked.

'He's thrilled by what's happening. He wants to watch the television news every night.'

'You're not thrilled?'

She looked at him as though she were wondering what he wanted to hear.

Of course she was thrilled. She had nothing to lose, she hadn't got mixed up in politics, she'd only sold things of slightly worse quality than things sold everywhere else in the world.

'They say there'll be private shops again,' she said, not replying directly. 'And they also say they're going to give people back their property, maybe even whole factories.'

'What's that got to do with us?'

'It's just that that's what they told us at head office.'

'My parents owned nothing, not even a kennel,' he said. 'They won't be giving anything back to me.'

'Nor to me, either. Unless they give Kučera back the factory his father used to own.' She sounded casual, but it was clear she had given the possibility a great deal of thought.

The telephone rang.

She stood up quickly and grabbed the receiver. He could hear a male voice on the other end asking a question. He saw that she was blushing. He got up, but there was nowhere for him to go, unless he went back into the shop, which was supposed to be empty.

'Call me tomorrow,' she said into the phone, unconsciously lowering her voice. 'I have a visitor.' She hung up quickly. 'That was him,' she said, 'Kučera. He wants to arrange to take Robin skiing.'

'So why didn't you make the arrangements?'

She shrugged her shoulders. 'I need some time to think about it.' She walked over to the desk, bent over and began rummaging for something in the bottom drawer.

He watched her half-exposed breasts, the breasts he had touched so often. He reached for her and took her in his arms.

She looked at him, surprised, but then let herself be kissed. 'Are you mad?' she said, when he began fondling her. 'We can't do it here . . . '

'But you've locked the door.'

'The boss has a key.'

'Do you think she might turn up?'

'And I have to go to the post office.'

He stroked her breasts.

'I don't know, I don't know.' But she didn't resist when he carried her to the chair.

She made love to him perfunctorily, silently and passively, probably because she didn't like the place.

'You make love to me, but you don't really like me,' she said as she was putting on her clothes.

'What makes you say that?'

'When was the last time you told me you loved me?'

'I love you.'

'But you don't want to have a baby with me.'

He said nothing.

'And you don't want to marry me.'

'But it's as though we're married.'

'Yes, you can have me any time you want. In the shop, on a chair, just because you happen to feel like it. But you're not interested in the rest of it. You're not interested in me. You're not interested in Robin either. You don't like either of us.'

'I have no idea why you're talking like this.'

'I've known for ages. I'm just telling you now. You only care about your mother and maybe your camera—at least you make bloody sure no one does *that* any harm.'

'Has anyone done you any harm?'

'Yes. You!'

'Here? Now?'

'Here or somewhere else. It doesn't matter where, you don't really love me. You think only about yourself.'

She went back to the desk and pushed the drawer shut. Then she took some lipstick out of her handbag and began to apply it carefully as she looked in the mirror. 'How long do you think I'm going to hang around waiting to see whether you've decided to stay with me or take up with someone else?'

'But I'm staying with you.'

'All the same, you're cheating on me. Don't think I don't know it.'

'I'm not cheating on you,' he said, without conviction. Her explosion had caught him off guard. Until now, she had submissively done things his way. Something must have happened. She was a real shopkeeper. She had it in her blood. The world around her was collapsing and re-arranging itself into something that could bring profit or loss or something else entirely.

Until now, he had represented profit to her. He was a better sort of companion than she could ever have hoped for. Either she had concluded that he could no longer bring her any advantage, or someone else had appeared who offered her better value. Or both of those things had happened, and he had failed to notice.

She got into her coat, glanced at herself in the mirror again and put on her hat. 'Shall we go?'

They were silent for most of the journey. As they were getting close to where she lived, he asked, 'Was there anything else you wanted to tell me?'

'Why? I've said all I want to say for the time being.'

4

PETER HAD TAKEN over from Halama and was now Pavel's new boss. Pavel didn't know whether this was good or not. On the surface, not much in his life had changed, but the certainty had gone out of it. He brought footage back from wherever they sent him, and then they broadcast it, without anyone either objecting or approving. He might tell himself that he had finally achieved independence and responsibility, but in fact the situation made him increasingly uneasy.

He even found it hard to concentrate on his tennis and lost three sets one morning to Sokol. In the showers, when Sokol remarked that the same old thing was starting up again, Pavel asked what he meant.

'You know, first they replace the bosses, then the bosses start replacing the ones underneath them and so it goes, all the way down. Except for the cleaning ladies. They get to stay,' he explained. 'Or maybe you think that's not how it's going to be this time?'

He shrugged his shoulders.

'They say this new guy spent years as a custodian of some castle,' Sokol informed him, 'and that he's a Catholic.'

'Protestant,' he corrected him.

'You know him?'

'A bit.'

'So what do you think he'll do?'

'I don't know. Maybe he doesn't know himself.'

'Maybe he'll ask you for advice, since you know each other.'

'I doubt it.'

'Or maybe you'll be the first to get fired?'

'I don't know. I really don't know.'

'What the hell does a glorified caretaker know about running a television network?'

'He wasn't always a caretaker.'

'Even so. The only thing he'll know for sure is that he's expected to replace us. It would be better not to wait. We'd be wasting our time, and now it's more true than ever that time is money. Have you thought at all about my idea of setting up an advertising agency? Remember, we talked about it? Do you have any idea what kind of money the ones who get in there first will make?'

Pavel shrugged. 'I don't understand why you want me to go in with you.' He'd already finished dressing. He didn't want to talk about it now. He was tired and thirsty after the game.

'A lot of empty buildings will be available now,' said

Sokol, sticking to his subject, 'and if we move quickly we can still get something pretty decent, something we can turn into a studio. It will cost a bit, but if several of us get together . . . '

'Why should anyone be in any hurry to give us a building?'

'They'll give it to whoever pays the most, that's how they operate. And if they don't happen to like you or me, we'll do it under someone else's name.'

'Perhaps. But why?'

'God,' sighed Sokol. 'Where do you think you're living? Don't you understand that everything has changed? If we stay in television, we'll always be the black sheep. But if we start out on our own, no one's going to ask us questions about our past, only about what we know and whether we can do the job.'

'I had a different idea about what I'd do when things changed.'

'A different idea?'

Pavel paused for a moment and then said, 'Like making a film that I really want to make.'

Sokol looked surprised. 'Your own film? And what, if I may ask, would it be about?'

'Did it never cross your mind?'

'What do you mean?'

'You know, that you might have your own way to say the things you always had to say their way?'

'Oh, sure,' he waved his hand. 'But now everybody's going to be doing that.'

'If they still can.'

'And you can pull it off?'

'I can at least try.'

'What about money? Where's that going to come from?'

'That remains to be seen.'

'Well, why not? We'll have a studio, and you can make your big film.' He liked the sound of the idea. 'It's probably the one place where you'll be able to do something like that.'

When he finally got back home, three weeks late (he was working all the time), Albina was no longer a patient at the hospital; she was back at work there.

He waited for her outside the hospital gate. He had a bag of nicely wrapped presents: a necklace of tiny turquoise stones, an alpaca sweater and two small silver pins, but the moment he saw her coming he realized, with a sinking feeling, that not even the most fantastic gifts would be of any help. She must have seen him too, but she didn't quicken her step and her face gave no sign that she was glad to see him.

'So you're back?' she said.

'I'm with you again,' he said, and tried to kiss her.

She pulled away. 'You're not with me, we're standing on the street.'

He wanted to walk her to his car but she refused to go.

'We're going somewhere,' he said.

'No we're not. I wasn't expecting you.'

'You weren't expecting me?'

'I wanted you to come, I wanted you to come a lot, but that was a month ago.'

He tried to explain that he couldn't come, that he had tried to phone her but couldn't get through. She said there was nothing to explain. It was entirely up to him whether he came back or not, and in the same way, it was entirely up to her whether she wanted to stay with him or be alone.

She got into the car with him in the end. She asked him how the trip had gone.

He tried again to explain that he hadn't stopped loving her, it was just that he hadn't been able to come back right away, but she insisted that there was nothing for him to explain. She had always known he would keep running away from her, and that one day he'd leave her for good; it was in him, or rather, there was something missing in him, something he lacked, and lacked so utterly that he wasn't even aware of it.

He asked her if she could at least say what that something was.

She thought for a while, then said that he lacked hope.

Hope for what?

Hope that something in life had real meaning. That life itself had some meaning.

It was odd that she spoke not of love nor of faith, but of hope.

What meaning did life have, then?

It meant, for instance, to be with the one you love when she needs you.

She wanted to get out of the car, but he persuaded her to stay a while longer. So they sat for another hour, but he was incapable of saying anything important. He even forgot to give her the presents he'd brought. But she'd have rejected them, leaving him with the feeling that he'd tried to bribe her. When she got out, she asked him not to phone her any more, or wait for her after work.

But he did try waiting for her for several days after that, although he knew he was waiting in vain. He knew it was all over.

Later that evening he ran into Halama's former secretary, who was now working for Peter. She had been looking for him since yesterday. Her new boss would like to talk to him.

'When?'

'This evening after work.'

'Which means when?'

'About nine. Every day. It's terrible, Pavel. I sit there with him, not because I have to, but because I'm afraid he'll think that I've been used to taking it easy. And I've got two kids at home screaming for their supper.'

'He'll get over it.' He went into the editing room to give them a tape of the ceremonial dismantling of the border fortifications. He poured himself a glass of red wine and sipped it slowly, smoking and looking at the screen.

Ministers and lesser representatives of the people were cutting the wire. It seemed soft and fell harmlessly to the ground with a snip of the wire-cutters. Something that concerned him directly was coming to an end. He rewound the tape. He couldn't concentrate. Why did Peter want to see him? Would he try to rub his nose in his triumph, or would he just be friendly? The government ministers on the monitor looked friendly, even human. In fact, they didn't look like ministers at all. This was a different breed of people from the old lot. How long would those expressions last?

Either their places would be taken by others, or their expressions would gradually adapt to fit their positions. There was still some time left before going to see Peter, but he was beginning to feel more and more uneasy.

Again he rewound the tape. He took a sip of wine. Of course, what had happened must have been a great source of satisfaction to Peter. He had laid linoleum floors, been a caretaker in a castle, endured interrogations, while he, Pavel, had spent his time making conformist documentaries, travelling the world and filming eulogies to the man who had run the country into the ground. In return, he was given bonuses and rewards, and from time to time he bought a bottle of wine and went down to see his friends in exile in their castle, and then only because he wanted to see Alice. And now his friend had summoned him and could grant him pardon, trust and work. Or not. There was something humiliating in this sudden transformation. Sokol was probably right: it would be better not to wait.

He stopped the tape, put his feet up on the control panel and lit a cigarette. In fact he had never received many bonuses because he'd never felt that he had to kowtow to the bosses the way those who weren't any good did. Instead, he would argue with them, refuse to cut what they wanted to cut. One Friday, at a weekly meeting of the chief producers, he said out loud what everyone was thinking: they were producing a mixture of blandness and tedium. And lies, he had wanted to add, but when he saw the expression on the director's face he swallowed the word. As a punishment, they assigned him to film meetings held by meaningless organizations, or official visits from their official, though hostile, allies. There were disgusting meetings, idiotic approval sessions when he had to sit and silently listen to drivel that often, in an instant, swept away days of work. The life he led was neither wonderful nor easy. Sometimes it had seemed unbearable. Like most people in this country, he'd done his job. He was one of the ones who got steamrollered daily, not one of the ones who drove the steamroller. He was overwhelmed with regret when he thought of what he might have done if they'd left him just a little freedom. He watched the delight on the faces of those who were cutting the wires and those who were merely looking on, and he realized that he had tears in his eyes.

A melancholy alcoholic who didn't know whether he was crying for joy or grief or anger, or simply because he had drunk himself into a state in which his eyes produced tears by themselves.

Peter looked tired. He was sitting in Halama's huge office, where nothing had changed but the picture of the president and the books on the shelves. Halama had either taken his books away or, more likely, thrown them out. He never read them anyway. One of the two television sets in the room was on, but the sound was down.

Peter got up and walked over to meet him. In the few months since they had last seen each other he had aged, and his face was sallow and wan.

'Have I kept you waiting long?'

'You've kept yourself waiting too.' Pavel's stomach was in a knot.

'I didn't want to talk to you for any particular reason, but it occurred to me that we're working under the same roof and haven't seen each other yet.'

'People who work here sometimes don't see each other for months at a time.'

'I have no intention of sounding you out about anyone.'

'I couldn't tell you much anyway. In my line of work, you make sure the lighting's right and you look through the viewfinder, not at the people around you.'

'That's a little hard to believe,' said Peter, 'but that's not the point. I know people are nervous.'

'Some are, some aren't.'

'They shouldn't be.'

'You don't think so?'

'It seems to me they haven't understood that this is different from the changes they've experienced in the past. No one is going to start any purges.'

'A couple of people have been sacked already.'

'That's different. They weren't real professionals, or else they broke the journalistic code of ethics. I mean, you can't expect people to accept an announcer beating the drum for democracy when the same person was beating the drum for the old regime a month ago. And you can't expect new programmes to be produced by old censors.' He was beginning to sound preachy.

'Most people here weren't beating the drum for anything. And it was us who argued with the censors, not you.'

'Almost all of us argued in one way or another. And how about you? Are you happy with your work?'

'No, I'm not. I can't concentrate the way I'd like to.'

'Why not?'

He shrugged. 'The atmosphere around here isn't very good.'

'It was good before?'

'No, but that was different. I'm sorry. You ask me, I answer. You said yourself there were people who were unethical. Who's doing the judging here? Who decides who's guilty? And what about me? What are they going to think about me?'

'I've already told you enough times what I think about you.'

'It was hardly flattering.'

'You know very well that I've never thought of myself as your judge. I know you too well for that.'

'You don't have to apologize. If you want me out of here, just say so.'

'I don't want you out of here, but if you don't feel comfortable here, I can't force you to stay.'

'I'm glad to hear you won't force me to stay.' He should have stood up now and brought this embarrassing conversation to a close.

But Peter began to talk about himself. He said he thought it was his responsibility to take the position when it was offered but now he felt like an interloper. Some hated him, some tried to suck up to him and others tried to curry favour with him by informing on their colleagues. Yet he had neither the inclination nor the desire to play the judge. We all lived in this country. Given the conditions that existed here, every one of us came out of it scarred in some way. And who can establish a borderline between guilt and innocence, when that borderline runs somewhere right down the middle of each and every person? People overthrew the old regime in the hope that they would finally see justice done. There would have to be an attempt at some kind of judgement. 'Someone can probably be found who can establish that borderline,' Peter said, 'but it won't be me. The job will probably be done by someone who will use it to cover up his own guilt.'

What was justice?

Justice was revenge wrapping itself in a cloak of high principle.

On television, the minister was now cutting the border wires. People behind him were cheering noiselessly. Peter looked at the screen for a moment: 'We tried to run away together once, remember?'

'That was a long time ago,' Pavel said.

'Was that really us? People meet, drift apart, and maybe they meet again, but by then they're someone else.'

Pavel nodded. 'Even so, they can still ride in the same car. That is if you're leaving too.'

When they got into his car, he said to Peter, 'I don't even know where you live now.'

'For the time being I'm living at my sister's.'

'What about Alice and the children?'

'She stayed in the country. I thought you knew.' He was silent for a long time as though wondering whether to come out with it. 'I got involved with someone else, a girl who writes poetry and sings. Alice was badly hurt. We separated.'

'I didn't know.'

It was a long time since he'd made that movie about children who had lost their fathers.

'I'm sorry,' he said. For the first time in days, he felt the unexpected touch of hope.

FILM

I

THE RECEPTION TAKES place in the small house which also serves as his private dwelling. Tables spread with white cloths are positioned throughout five rooms. There are tables outside as well, in the parts of the garden adjacent to the house, but it still seems crowded in here. He has invited too many spongers. All those cheap suits, black faces and slant-eyed devils milling about. Wherever he looks he sees freeloaders, tinpot attachés in toy uniforms, overdressed cannibals, decorated warriors, retired admirals and failed generals, ambassadors from postage-stamp, god-forsaken kingdoms and hordes of would-be artists: actors, musicians and hacks. They brought him a guest list, but he was exhausted before he finished reading the first page, so he signed it, just as he'd signed hundreds of other documents. He knows there are people here who were not on the list, people disguised in tuxedos and waiters' frock-coats, dressed up as gardeners, cooks, lighting experts and television cameramen spread out on all sides of him, creating an impenetrable circle around him.

He's sitting in a small salon off the main rooms. They wedge him in among his special black guests on tiny rococo chairs and ply him with caviar, alcohol, delicious salads, crab meat, stuffed artichokes, shrimps. An ugly, bespectacled interpreter is standing just behind him, droning on and on in her high, wheezing voice. As soon as that cannibal to his left flaps her thick painted lips three times and utters a few incomprehensible sounds, the woman behind him dumps a load of words on him so rapidly he can't concentrate on a single thought of his own. Fortunately, they've trained him how to behave in situations like this. Every once in a while he throws out a 'How interesting!' and smiles. Then he turns to her spouse, recommends that he try a sip of his favourite drink, then raises his glass and proposes that they drink to the struggle against capitalism, colonialism, neocolonialism, Zionism, racism, apartheid; to the war against poverty, hunger, illiteracy, corruption, crime, disease and exploitation. And when his guest, a huge man who lounges in the imperial chair as if to the manner born, as if, not so long ago, he hadn't lounged about on the banks of the Nile, or whatever river it was, among the hippopotamuses and the crocodiles, nods patronizingly to indicate that yes, he approves of such toasts, the president empties his glass and then announces that to add spark to the programme he has prepared something a little unorthodox. Given his guest's legal training, he might perhaps be interested in the case of a terrorist, who, with a second terrorist, hijacked a bus full of children. He's already been sentenced and has naturally been given the greatest punishment, but before he makes a decision on the man's request for clemency, he wants to hear him out personally. A thousand years ago his predecessors did things the same way. He had intended to have the hijacker brought to him some time in the next few days, but because of his guest, he has decided to do it right here and now.

The black guest nods, emits some incomprehensible sounds which the interpreter puts into comprehensible words strung together in utterly confused sentences. What does it matter? He is not here, after all, to contemplate the ruminations of someone whose parents grew up in the jungle. He'll show him the prisoner. Let his guest see for himself that all the talk about the horrors of unfreedom and biased courts in this country is merely the slander of malevolent enemies. He'll show him an outcast justly condemned to death. He will then talk to this outcast and hear what he has to say. He understands people like that because he has been a hair's breadth from the gallows himself. Where else in the world can you find the head of a civilized state willing to do that? He has even had a special room prepared for the event. That is, if his staff have obeyed his orders and brought him the chair in which his predecessors used to sit a thousand years ago. Then he will decide. He might even grant the prisoner clemency. Why shouldn't he? The world holds mercy in higher regard than punishment, however just. He can point to this act of mercy when his enemies malign him. He is only exercising his rightful powers. Besides, he who grants clemency holds power firmly; he rules. They know that very well, which is why some of them made rather sour faces when they understood his purpose.

He has worked the whole thing out wonderfully well, and feels satisfied with himself. He feels the old determination surging through his veins. He's even being a good host. 'Make yourself at home,' he says turning to his black guests, 'as though you were with your own people. All of this is yours. Let friendship flourish between us and the people of our countries, today, tomorrow and forever!' As he says this he looks into the garden where, over the heads of all those fancy-dressed scarecrows out there, geysers of colourfully lit waters explode into the air. 'No more the horrors of war, colonialism and subjugation!' He listens contentedly as his interpreter translates his pointed and comprehensible words into wads of shrill, inhuman sounds. 'For a free tomorrow, and against all those who would suck people dry and lead them astray,' he goes on. 'No more the rule of lords or clerics . . . '

His big-eared chancellor, who is sitting just close enough not to miss a word, is shaking his head almost imperceptibly. What is he trying to tell him? Probably that this black charlatan is, on top of everything else, an archbishop or a shaman, if not some kind of local deity, and that he should be careful not to offend him. Has it reached the point when he has to watch what he says and what he thinks in his own home, in his own country?

He lifts the goblet to his lips (the chancellor watching him closely) and takes a modest sip. He should probably change the subject, otherwise this treacherous little runt of a chancellor will get upset. He should try to tell an amusing story. After they let him out of prison, he worked in the props department of a theatre, where he heard hundreds of stories. He told many himself. He could tell the story of how they arrested him at gunpoint, except that in the land of cannibals in pinstriped suits that kind of thing probably happens every day. In fact, they don't even arrest people there, they just shoot them. That way they can be certain that their opponents will never come back to haunt them. So he sticks to stories about how they prepared the props for a traditional farce set in the mountains. In one scene, the brigands were returning to their mountain hide-out and as they passed through the entrance, each one was supposed to embed his axe in a wooden beam overhead. The beam had a facing of soft wood, and before the performance it was soaked in water so that the axes would go into it more easily. The actor who played the leading robber was a police spy and an informer of whom everyone was terrified. One day, when the president was dressing the set for the performance, he turned the beam over so that the soft wood was on the back and when the robber chieftain came on stage and casually swung his axe into the wood, it bounced off and fell to the floor. The actor bent over, picked it up and this time took a proper swing, but again the axe would not go into the wood, and by this time the whole theatre was rocking with laughter.

When he finishes telling his story, the black potentate stares blankly at him without so much as a grin. He probably only understands stories about cannibalism. The chancellor is also looking rather uneasy, and so the president raises his glass, which one of those conspirators in disguise has refilled, and he is so excited by his own story that he downs it all at once. His guest also takes a drink and looks satisfied. Apparently the savage understands good drink. He should ask him what they drink back home in his country, on the banks of the Nile or wherever he's from. He should also ask him what he was before they made him a champion of peace and people's rights. He was probably a non-commissioned officer who got together with a few like him, staged a successful uprising and then named himself and his comrades-in-arms generals. But at least his generals had proved themselves in battle, he thinks bitterly, and he's got a good-looking wife too. They didn't get rid of her. He was able to keep a closer eye on his wife than I was on mine, though he may have more than one. Perhaps he has a whole harem, in which case it wouldn't make sense to eliminate just one. They would have to invent accidents for all of them, and that is not easy to do.

He recalls his own poor wife, and how they had all rushed to tell him about the accident, an accident they themselves had planned so carefully and executed so flawlessly that nothing could be proven. He was too devastated even to have them prosecuted, and no one was punished.

He reaches for his glass but they have forgotten to fill it, or rather have been ordered not to fill it any more. It's that scoundrel of a chancellor who has given the order and now he's smirking at him. Of course, he's made mistakes, he'll admit that. He tossed back that last drink just like in the old days, but couldn't they just forgive him that one slip, instead of leaving him stranded here? He could of course order another drink from one of those fellows disguised as a waiter, but they would criticize him first thing tomorrow morning for lack of self-control, and his enemies would be more than happy to exploit his lapse.

He looks around in the vain hope that someone will come to his rescue. But who could he expect to do that? And why haven't they brought him that criminal yet?

Have they even prepared the room as he'd ordered them to? With the special chair in the middle, and twenty-two seats in a square around it for the guests? Have they remembered to get the robe ready? He should check on it at once; they can't be depended on for anything. He's all alone, surrounded by enemies. He knows who they are. Some of them are staggering tipsily around him, others are lurking among the Chinese vases or concealed behind heavy curtains, behind the firescreen, behind secret doors, all of them perfectly disguised in suits and white shirts, their bodies creating a net so dense that not even a little bird could fly through, and they have hidden hooks in their trouser-legs. When he looks around with his heightened vision, he realizes there are more of them now. On the opposite wall, under the enormous tapestry depicting a scene of debauchery between a naked woman and a swan, two pairs of black shoes peep out. He sees that a tiny, almost invisible door in one of the bookshelves is open, a sinister eye peering through the crack. His heightened senses pick up the sour odour of the deviousness molecule in the air. They are undoubtedly planning something, weaving some treachery around him. Now he must be especially watchful. He must not be caught off his guard, yet he must conceal the fact that he has seen through their designs.

He who grants pardon also has the right to mete out punishment. Suppose that when he grants clemency to the hijacker, he also punishes some of these layabouts who so perfidiously pretend to be his friends?

He hopes they haven't forgotten to hang up the antique banner. He gets up to check, but before he has gone more than a few steps he hears a metallic scraping at his back as though they were stealthily sharpening knives. He turns around abruptly and sees the chancellor, that devious hyena, huddling in treasonous conversation with the minister of the interior, his chief enemy and pretender to his position. The two of them suddenly spring apart, grinning hypocritically. But he pretends that he hasn't even seen them and goes back to his place among the savages.

Before he's able to sit down, the Judas chancellor waltzes up to him on his chickenlike legs and puts on an extremely gloomy expression. As soon as the chancellor addresses him, he knows that he is getting ready to present him with a freshly plucked flower of deception.

'Mr President, I've just learned some rather unpleasant news.' His satisfaction is evident in his voice, although he is trying to conceal it. 'The granting of clemency will have to be rescheduled.' And before the president is able to ask the chancellor why he wants to spoil the plan, the scoundrel informs him that the car bringing the hijacker to him has been involved in an accident. The escorts have been fatally injured, and the hijacker has temporarily absconded.

'The guards are dead?'

The chancellor nods and mentions names and details. So, they did have a plan after all. It was their favourite trick—a traffic accident. It worked before, so now they're going to work it to death. More new victims, and then they'll bring them all in here to haunt him. He could expect them any moment now. This time they killed off the guards too, and it will be left to him to decorate them posthumously, sign letters of condolence to the widows and arrange for their personal pensions. All this, just to frustrate his plans, to diminish him in front of this savage, who is now glancing at him with malicious glee, as though he already knows what they have done. And he can't even have them prosecuted. In any case, who would he prosecute? There is nothing he can do but wait for them to arrange a traffic accident for him too.

'It's unpleasant,' the chancellor drones, 'but it must not be allowed to cast a shadow over the evening.' He snaps his fingers at one of the lackeys, who moves in quickly with a tray bearing a glass of his favourite drink, golden and aromatic. That's something at least—this miserable little fox is trying to mollify him. He grasps the glass, and though the tiny amount of golden liquid scarcely quenches his thirst, it gives him a jolt and he remembers something else. 'What about that other fellow?'

He watches with delight as the devious little runt squirms in embarrassment, vainly searching for an excuse.

'Was this another case of clemency?' the chancellor enquires tightly.

'Yes. And a film,' he remembers, 'a film about snakes.' The chancellor is just about to unleash a torrent of the usual pretexts, but this time he has miscalculated, he's underestimated him, failed to observe that today, the old determination is flowing through his veins. 'Why isn't that fellow here? How dare you not bring him?'

The runt bows his head. He's so small now that all he would have to do would be to lift his leg and . . .

'Bring him here!' the president orders. 'And bring me the other one too, the one who's hiding, the terrorist. Use all means necessary! And I mean all! Right away!'

At last he has managed to foil them.

II

IT'S DARK. ROBERT crouches in the bushes by the wall, as hungry and thirsty as a runaway dog. His leg is hurting.

It's high time he had a roof over his head, somewhere nearby. He mustn't be seen on the streets. The best thing would be to hole up for a couple of days in one of those blocks of flats on the other side of the wall.

He scans the lit windows. One looks possible, the second on the left on the third floor of the middle block. The lights have just gone on and he sees a colourfully painted ceiling. The walls are covered floor to ceiling with photographs. A blonde girl appears in the window and stares out into the darkness for a while. He waits to see if there's a man with her, but no, she seems to be alone. He watches her as she wanders about the room.

It's getting late. It's Friday evening. He has to get moving before they lock the apartment building. He climbs the low wall and drops down on the other side. A narrow path leads through the bushes. He hopes that no one will be using it at this hour. In the moonlight he can see the grey walls of the prefabricated buildings in front of him, a battery of dustbins and empty sandboxes. He has to get this right. He scans the windows, the courtyards and the end of the path. Not a soul.

When he walks across the open space around the building, he tries not to limp. With only a step or two to go, the door to the next block of flats opens, releasing a shaft of light. He sees a puffy face, a piglike neck throttled by an olive collar. A uniform of some kind. He notices all this in the fraction of a second before he grasps the door handle and pulls. Thank God, it's not locked. The dank corridor swallows him up. He has no idea whether that bastard outside noticed him or not. Maybe he couldn't see much, since he was coming from the light into darkness. He walks up a foul-smelling staircase. They've probably had his picture all over the television, so that fellow must have been curious about a stranger entering a neighbouring building by the back door. He should probably get the hell out of here. But if this fellow has called the police, there's nothing much he can do about it.

Third floor, second door from the left, a card with a handwritten name on it under the bell:

VALENTOVÁ

He rings the bell twice and waits. He hears a muffled woman's voice: 'Just a moment.' A door slams. He hears a lavatory flushing.

Someone is coming up the stairs. If it's the uniform coming after him, he's not going to pull any punches. He knows how to handle people like him, and he's got nothing to lose.

He hears light footsteps on the other side of the door. One floor below, a key turns in a lock. Someone is bound to hear him. The door opens.

She's not exactly a girl; she's probably older than he is. Not bad-looking. Earrings dangle from her lobes. She's wearing a short-sleeved sweater and a worn skirt and clogs. He notices a blue-and-white nurse's uniform on a coat-hanger behind her. 'Good evening. Sister Valentová?'

'Yes, that's me.' She stares at him, trying to remember if she's seen him somewhere before.

'I've got a message for you.'

'Who from?'

She's not blonde, as he'd thought seeing her from a distance. She's wearing a yellow scarf around her head. Her eyes are like his: large and dark blue.

'I've been on the train all day,' he said—the door on the floor below finally closes—'and I've come straight here from the station.'

'And what is it you have to tell me at this time of night?'

'It'll take a while. But first, I wonder could I trouble you for a glass of water?' He speaks slowly, calmly, choosing his words carefully. But the woman is nervous.

'I don't know you,' she says, 'and I'm not expecting a message from anyone. If you have something to say, say it, but you can't come in.'

Why bother with manners? The woman is going to start screaming any minute now. He has no time to waste. He offers her his hand and says, 'My name is Pavel.' He grasps her hand and pushes her into the flat, closing the door behind him with his other hand.

'You . . . you . . . Leave at once . . . or I'll . . . '

'Don't be afraid of me,' he says quickly, 'I won't hurt you. Now, get me something to drink.'

'You haven't got a message for me. What do you want?'

'Didn't you hear what I said? I'm thirsty. Can't you get me a glass of water?'

'Over there,' she says pointing to a door. 'If you're thirsty, get yourself a drink and then leave. Otherwise I'm going to start screaming.'

'Thanks, but you're coming with me.'

'No, I'm going to stay here by the door,' she says, raising her voice. 'You can have a drink, but then you have to go.'

'Listen to me,' he says quietly. 'You want to know where I'm from . . . I've just escaped from the slammer.' He pushes her in front of him into the room with posters and photographs all over the walls. 'Now I've got to stay here and you've got to stay with me.'

'You're mad.'

'If you keep your head and stay nice and quiet, nothing's going to happen to you.' He opens the door. The bathroom is small. There is a blue toothbrush in a yellow glass. 'If you shout . . . ' he says, and very lightly he brings his hand close to her throat. He stares for a moment into her eyes, which are wide with terror and, without taking his eyes off her, he turns the glass upside down. The toothbrush tumbles to the floor. He turns on the tap and holds the glass under the stream of water.

'Who are you?' Her voice is trembling.

'It doesn't matter a damn.'

'What do you want? What do you want from me?'

'Nothing!' He was holding a full glass of water. 'I've got to stay here with you for a little while.' He gulps down the cool liquid.

'You can't! There's someone coming to see me soon.'

She's lying, of course. He can see that she's lying. 'Rubbish!'

'There is someone coming.'

'So, you won't answer the door.'

'He has a key.'

'If he gets in, that's his bad luck.'

'You can't stay here,' she repeats doggedly.

'I've had bugger-all to eat since morning. Where do you keep your food?'

'If I give you something to eat, will you go?'

'I'll go,' he promises. 'That's the last you'll ever hear of me.'

She pulls back a pink curtain. There's an electric hot-plate on a shelf and beside it a bread bin, a frying-pan, a green saucepan, several tins and a jar of jam. She opens a tiny refrigerator and takes out a hunk of bacon and two eggs. 'That's all I've got.'

'That'll do.'

She turns on the hotplate and sets the frying-pan on it. Then she cuts the bacon into slices and throws it into the pan.

He breathes in the aroma. 'If you don't try anything funny, I won't touch you. Trust me.'

'When did you escape?'

'You don't want to know.'

She breaks the eggs into the sizzling fat.

He swallows impatiently. 'How about a slice of bread?'

She opens the bread bin and pulls out a wretched little slice.

'That's it?'

'It's enough for me.' She fishes out a plate from under the plastic curtain and dumps the contents of the frying-pan on to it. In the other room, she spreads a cloth on a small table. The cloth is white, with a reddish stain in one corner, probably from wine, but it annoys him and he sits so that he can't see it. He lifts a forkful of food to his mouth, but it's so hot it brings tears to his eyes. The bread is as hard as it was in solitary. He knows she was lying when she told him she was expecting someone.

She stands as far away from him as she can. 'When you've finished, you have to go. Really, you do. I beg you.'

'OK, I'll go, but first I need a change of clothes,' he says with his mouth full.

'There's nothing here for you to change into.'

'He's got his own key and he doesn't even leave his socks?'

'Besides, I have to go to the hospital. I'm on duty.'

'Where do you work?'

'In surgery.'

'Great. You can take a look at my leg. It got a bit of a knock as I was getting away.'

'You can't stay here,' she says. 'And anyway, someone is bound to hear us. The walls are like paper.'

'Then we'll have to whisper, won't we?' he says quietly and gives her a look that makes the woman nod quickly. He mustn't frighten her too much, though. He needs her to help him get out of this town, whatever the name of it is, and help him get a car and go with him when he heads for the wire again. 'You wouldn't turn me in, would you?'

'You promised you'd leave!' She was really whispering now.

'I'll be gone by morning. I've got to get out of this gear or they'll be on to me before I'm out of the building.'

Her cupboard is plastered with posters too. Inside there are several skirts, a few brightly coloured dresses, another nurse's uniform and a pair of jeans. One shelf holds tall, neat piles of sweaters and sheets. There are several boxes on the floor of the cupboard, probably shoes.

He takes the jeans off the hanger. Original Levi's. They look as though they'll fit him—the gourmet prison cooking had taken care of that—but the legs will be too short. He looks at one of them. It has a deep hem. 'Let these down for me,' he says.

'They're the only ones I have. I can't afford to replace them.'

'I'll send you a new pair. I'll send you two pairs. The minute I'm out of here.'

'They'll get you sooner or later.'

'Not alive, they won't.' He should have added they wouldn't get her alive either, but he doesn't want to frighten her. He tosses her the jeans and then reaches into the pile of sweaters and picks out one that he thinks looks the least feminine. He takes off his jacket and only now notices that it's torn at the back and stained with blood. He pulls the sweater on. The sleeves are too short, but he rolls them up. It won't quite reach the top of his trousers, but it'll do. She holds the jeans in her hands, staring at him.

'What are you gaping at? Get on with it!'

She gets up and pulls a box of sewing things from under the bed. Some shoes would come in handy, but he doubts he'll find any here. Even so, he bends down and opens one of the boxes in the bottom of the cupboard. He almost shouts for joy at what he finds. He'd never have thought of this. Now he's beginning to believe he might get away.

'It's real hair,' he hears the woman say behind him. 'Don't take it, please. I have to wear it. I've lost my hair.'

Ignoring her, he stands in front of the mirror and tries on the wig. It's slightly fairer than his own hair and fits him well. It's too long, but a pair of scissors will fix that. Now, with long hair, in these clothes, arm in arm with this bird, he could walk right up to them and ask them the way to the station.

'I'm only borrowing it. I'll send it back to you, special delivery.' He watches her pull out the stitches around the hem of one trouser-leg and feels hopeful. He's got a roof over his head, he's here with a woman he can reach out and touch whenever he wants. As a matter of fact, he can do whatever he feels like with her. He might have been strung up by now, lying stretched out somewhere, stiff and cold. Instead, it's his escorts who are stiff and cold. 'I owe you one. I'll send you things, stuff like you've never seen before.'

'You think so . . . What did they lock you up for anyway?'

'For shit,' he snaps. 'I just wanted to get over those hills.'

'That was it?'

'That was enough.'

'I knew someone like that once.' She stops, then adds: 'He was a patient of ours, on the surgical floor. He tried to escape too. They gave him almost two years for it . . . '

The conversation is going nowhere. 'Have you got any cigarettes?'

She hesitates, then reaches for her handbag on the couch beside her. She hands him a packet and a box of matches.

He lights a cigarette, inhales the smoke hungrily and looks her up and down. Good-looking. A bit skinny, but nice tits. Christ, when was the last time he'd had a woman? But he mustn't scare her. Maybe she'll give in of her own accord. They usually did in the end. But if she starts screaming now, or later when he takes her with him . . . No, he mustn't scare her. When it's all over, when he's made it out of here, he'll have all the women he wants.

She hands him the jeans. 'There . . . and now you can . . . ' She doesn't feel like repeating herself, so she simply points to the door. 'I really mean it. Please.'

He gets up and takes off his trousers. His left ankle is swollen and dark blue, as though he's poured ink over it.

She notices this. 'You made it this far on that?'

'So?' he says, 'What was I supposed to do? Take a taxi?'

'You need to put it in plaster, at least.'

'Fuck that.' He reaches for the jeans.

'Wait a minute.' She fetches a box from the cupboard. She takes a bandage out of it and then she grasps his ankle and moves his foot around. It feels as if she were prising open his leg, but he doesn't let out a peep, he doesn't even move.

She unwinds the bandage with nimble fingers. 'Are they after you?'

'Now what do you think?'

'And when they catch you?'

'They'll tie me up here,' and he circles his throat with his thumb and forefinger and sticks out his tongue. 'But like I say, they won't catch me alive.'

'You're not serious.'

He says nothing.

'Are you in for . . . Did you . . . ?'

'I told you, I'm in for shit. No, I didn't kill anybody. If I had, they'd never have caught me. But I was stupid.'

'What are you going to do now? Where are you going to go?'

'We'll see. But I won't make the same stupid mistake twice, I can tell you that right now.'

She winds the bandage around his leg and finishes at his knee. Her head is close to his thigh. Unable to stop himself, he places his hand on her shoulder.

She jumps back as though he had scalded her. 'Keep your filthy hands off me!'

'Shut the fuck up!' He takes a step towards her, but he can scarcely move his leg. 'I wasn't, I wasn't going to . . . '

He deliberately turns his back on her and puts on her jeans. They're a bit tight, and he can barely pull them over his bandaged ankle, but otherwise they're all right. He runs some water into the sink and splashes himself. The lump on his forehead has gone down a little, and the wig will hide the scar that runs around to his right temple. He comes back for the wig and puts it on. 'It needs a trim,' he says.

'What'll you think of next?'

'Get me a pair of scissors.'

'No! Please!'

He reaches for the box with the sewing things, takes a pair of scissors, trims some hair off the wig and puts it on again in front of the mirror. How could they possibly recognize him now?

'And now will you get out of here?' she says behind him. 'You should be glad that they haven't caught you yet.'

'Let me worry about that.' She's probably right, though. He's got more than he hoped for here and now he should clear out as fast as he can before they sniff him out, before that uniformed bastard starts thinking about what he saw, or that busybody on the floor below wonders who was talking to her.

But what about this woman? Is she so stupid that she doesn't realize he can't just walk out and leave her? The minute he leaves she'll run to the nearest police station and start talking. He's got to persuade her to go with him. But what if he can't? Or what if she says she will and then starts screaming once they're out in the street? He hasn't thought that one through yet.

He lights another cigarette and sits down. Even if he left her here, gagged her and tied her up, they'd still find her. So he'll have to finish her . . . But he doesn't want to do that, and it wouldn't be that much use, because they'd find out something was missing from her wardrobe and then they'd know what to look for.

The woman wants to get up, but he motions her to stay sitting down. 'There's something else I've got to tell you.' She lights a cigarette, pulls the chair away slightly and sits down.

'It's funny,' he says, 'but I didn't catch the name of this metropolis of yours on my way in. How far is it from here to there?'

'To where?'

'To the wire.'

'It's a long way. You'd never make it.'

'What, an hour?'

'It depends on how you're travelling.'

'By car.'

'You've got one?'

'I will have.'

'About an hour.'

'Good. We can go!'

'"We"?'

'You're going with me.'

'No! No!' She jumps out of the chair, probably about to run into the corridor and start screaming. He grabs her shoulder and puts his other hand over her mouth. 'Sit down,' he orders. There's a knife lying beside the bread bin, the one she'd used to slice the bacon. He picks it up, tests the sharpness with his thumb. It's not too bad, so he sticks it into the back pocket of his jeans.

'Now look. You're going with me and you're going to pretend that we're together. It'll be OK. If you cooperate. But if you don't, it won't.' He pulls the knife out of his pocket and again runs his thumb over the sharp edge. 'Understand?'

She looks at him, not daring to move. 'You bastard,' she whispers.

He doesn't respond. He's heard some noises outside. Very cautiously, he gets up from the chair and goes over to the window.

It's incredible. How could they have sniffed him out? But there they are. Two of them, with dogs. He jumps back from the window.

'What is it?' she asks, and then she looks out. 'Are they after you?'

He can hear the dogs barking. He's blown it. He's wasted too much time here, hanging around chatting.

'So go,' he hears her say behind him. 'What are you waiting for? Do you want them to find you here?'

'Shut up!'

Where to now? Maybe up to the attic and then on to the roof, but he wouldn't get far with his fucked-up leg. And anyway they've got the place surrounded. He can hear their cars pulling up and he can picture them, each one with a gun in his hand and grenades in his pocket. But they won't get him that easily. It's a good thing she's here. They won't fool him this time. Either he and the woman leave in a car provided by them, or they'll have to carry both of them out of here in coffins.

'What is it?' She's shrieking at him now. 'What are you looking at me like that for? What are you going to do?'

'Shut up!'

'Just get out!' she shouts and she tries to push him towards the door. 'You can't stay here. You're not going to wait until they find you here.'

He hits her across the face. 'Get back, get back in there.' He points to the bed.

She holds her cheek and sobs.

A door slams and they hear feet pounding up the stairs. How many of them have stayed outside? He should keep away from the window now, do something. Barricade the doors. 'Come on!'

She gets up obediently. 'Let me go, can't you at least let me go?' she pleads. 'Maybe they're going to shoot.'

'They won't shoot as long as you're here. Help me with this thing.' He pushes the cupboard that's plastered with photographs and slides it towards the front door.

'Let me go, please, let me go. I haven't done anything to you!'

Only a little bit more effort and the door will be a lot harder to open. Footsteps at the top of the stairs.

'Let me go or I'll scream.'

'Go ahead and scream,' he says. 'Let them know you're in here with me.'

He jams the cupboard against the door. There, now

they're here together. Will the police dare do what they did then? He remembers the moment, the whistling bullets, the groans of the man behind the wheel. His forehead is beaded with sweat. 'Go on—scream!' he says. 'Why aren't you screaming?'

The footsteps stop outside the door. The buzzer sounds. The dogs are yelping and snarling; they sound ready to chew their way through the door. The buzzer goes again.

What is this? Are they here on a visit? They have guns in their hands, dogs at their sides, grenades in their pockets and they're ringing the bell? Maybe they don't want to disturb anyone. They'd rather he opened the door, bowed and then politely put up his hands. But that won't happen. They can find him here lying dead, but he'll make damn sure that his hands are by his side.

He leans against the pictures stuck to the door of the cupboard. The woman beside him is trembling and sobbing loudly. Let them hear her; at least they'll know she's here before they begin to shoot. Where will it come from? Through the door? Through the window? But there's nowhere they could take up a position opposite the window, unless it's on the roof of that warehouse where he'd taken shelter earlier that day. But they probably won't shoot. They'll break down the door and a whole platoon of them will force their way in. But they won't get him alive. He reaches into his pocket and feels the knife for re-assurance. This time they won't trick him. He won't even talk to them. Not a word!

Suddenly the buzzer stops, and even the dogs are quiet. Maybe they've taken them away. She's beside him, her shoulders trembling. 'Let them in,' she whispers, 'There's no point. Let them in.'

'Ask them what they want.'

'They want to get in.'

'I'm not asking you, bitch.'

She turns her head towards the cupboard, opens her mouth and then closes it again.

'Go on, ask them!'

'Who is it?' she says in a faint voice.

'Speak up, damn it!'

'Who's there?'

He hears some male voices. Then a strange, yet familiar voice, the same voice that had yelled at him in the children's home and in the army and in prison. 'Security. Open up!'

She turns to him. She's pale and her earrings are trembling.

'Say you won't open up. Say you're a hostage.'

She repeats his words.

'Say I'm going to kill you.'

Silence.

'Say I'll kill you if they don't give us a car and let us out.'

Silence.

'Say something, bitch!'

She sobs.

A voice from outside: 'Bartoš. We know you're inside. Open up!'

'Repeat what I said, bitch, or I'll kill you.'

'He says that he'll kill me if you don't let us leave.'

'Bartoš, the president of the republic has decided to grant you clemency. It's in your own interest not to do anything to make him change his mind.'

'Tell them they're a bunch of fucking liars.'

Silence. The woman's whole body is shaking, and she's sobbing. She turns her moist face to him. One cheek is beginning to swell. 'Leave me alone. Let me go.'

He bursts out laughing. They sentenced him to death when he hadn't hurt a soul, when he let all those kids go free on the strength of a promise. Now, when he's sent a whole carload of escorts to hell, they're granting him clemency. Maybe they think the car went out of control on a slippery road. That makes him want to laugh even more. He laughs so hard that they must be able to hear him outside. Let them know how much he's enjoying this.

'Bartoš, I'll give you three minutes to open up.'

He laughs.

'Then we'll break the door down.'

'Bartoš? Were you the one who hijacked that school

bus?' She looks at him in astonishment. 'Let me go. You let them go.'

'That was the stupidest thing we ever did. If they touch that door . . . ' He pulls out the knife and holds it up in front of her face. 'Go on, tell them what will happen.'

'Two more minutes, Bartoš.'

He puts the knife away. 'Tell them!'

'For God's sake, please go away. Leave us alone. He'll kill me.'

'Bartoš, if you lay a finger on that woman, you won't get out of here alive.'

He laughs.

'Tell them to get lost. I want a car for the two of us and I want a green light all the way to the line.'

'It's your last minute, Bartoš.'

'Let me go, you're crazy, they'll never give you a car, but they will give you clemency. You heard them.'

He laughs. 'Clemency?'

'I have an old mother. She's alone and she's sick. Let me go. It's not my fault they want you . . . please. I've given you food. I've bandaged your leg. I could have called for help, but I didn't want to betray you.'

He laughs.

'I felt sorry for you. I feel sorry for you now. I'd like to help you if I could but . . . '

'Keep your fucking mouth shut, you stupid bitch.'

'Bartoš, your time is up!'

They begin fiddling with the lock.

He grabs her arm, twists it and pulls her away.

'My God, he's going to kill me! Help! Help!'

He puts his hand over her mouth and tries to drag her away from the door.

She resists. She tries to kick him and bite him. He twists her arm harder, and now she really starts screaming, in real terror. He pushes her in front of him into another room. He hits her so hard she falls over, and the kerchief flies off her head. She has almost no hair. He turns away, disgusted, and closes the door and locks it.

He hears something snapping in the hallway but he doesn't care any more. If they want him they can have him.

He flings himself on her and grabs her throat. She kicks, she pounds at his stomach, scratches his face, but he is scarcely aware of it. He doesn't care. Nothing matters any more. He throws her to the floor, digs his knees into her breasts, grabs that strange hairless head and begins pounding it against the floor. The body beneath him thrashes about and groans. It makes him even more furious and he pounds it like a madman. Finally, she stops struggling and is silent. He pulls out the knife and holds it against her throat. He'll wait for them in this position so they'll see that all it will take is a single movement . . .

He can hear them now, outside the door, the whine of a drill.

He looks into the woman's blank face. Her pale forehead is wet with sweat. She's not moving. What if he's overdone it? What good is a dead hostage? He leans down and tries to hear her breathing, but he can't hear anything over the hellish buzzing of the drill.

Fear chokes him, and he shudders with the cold. They've got him after all. He didn't escape them. He shakes her lifeless head. *Speak, say something.* This is not what he wanted. He just wanted to get away from here, where everyone . . . where no one ever . . . Hc was always . . . like now: completely alone. It wasn't me, it was them, so you shouldn't think that I . . . the key on the floor behind him, another couple of seconds and then they'll drag him off to the waiting gallows, but they won't get him alive. He stares at the knife, which won't save him now unless he stabs himself with it, but suddenly he doesn't have the strength, he doesn't even know where to plunge in the blade. But the window's open. You can all kiss my arse. I shit on your world. And as though he were scaling a very low wall, he climbs on to the window-sill, not looking down but staring straight ahead, the warehouse roof and the dark sky beyond, a sky without stars. He takes a single step, a quite ordinary step, as though he had solid ground under him, as though he were still running, continuing on his impossible journey to cross the uncrossable line.

III

FUKA IS ASLEEP in his mother's flat when the telephone wakes him up. He fumbles for the receiver. 'Who is it?'

'Darling, it's me, Ella. Thank God you're there. They're waiting for you . . . '

'Who's waiting for me? You're crazy to call me with them listening.'

'It's not them. Not the ones you think. They're supposed to take you to him.'

'Where?'

'To the Castle. To the president. Just like I told you. He's going to receive you!' Ella is shouting.

'When?'

'Now, right now.'

'I'm not going anywhere. I just want to sleep. I didn't ask you to do this.'

'Darling, we're coming round for you right away. We'll be there shortly.'

He splashes some water on his face. It's almost one in the morning. This is truly insane. Perhaps he's only dreaming, or perhaps it's just a stupid joke. He doesn't know whether to go back to bed or put on his best suit. He goes to the window and stares out into the empty street. He looks at the wet cobblestones glistening in the glow of the streetlights. Then the glare of car headlights swings into the street and a black limousine pulls up in front of his house. A man jumps out, opens the back door and Ella steps out to bring him the good news in person.

He goes to get dressed.

Two men are waiting for him beside the car. To him, they are indistinguishable from the men who had recently checked his ID and confiscated his film. They have grey faces and are dressed in black, but this time they flash their teeth in a smile of official warmth. Apologetically, they ask to see his ID and they look pleased to confirm that it's really him. They put him in the back seat and drive off immediately, leaving Ella on the pavement, waving. She's delighted, for after all it was her idea, her contact, and she believes that his fortunes, and therefore her own fortunes, will now improve. He will get work, the work will bring him money, the money will buy them a house, the house will make them happy and she'll finally have him all to herself.

He settles into the back seat and watches the city go by. He doesn't know how long the journey will take. He doesn't even know what he's going to say to the head of state, if he really does get a hearing. Or what he will request. Although he tries not to admit it to himself, he's excited. It's as though Satan himself had invited him to a mountaintop and let him gaze down upon all the world's riches.

All this is yours.

Yes. But how shall I ever repay you, O Prince of Darkness?

We'll talk about that later.

No, I need to know now. Do you want loyalty? My freedom? My life? My soul?

The car turns on to a narrow, sandy road. It stops in front of a gateway, the wrought-iron gate opens, they go down a sand-covered drive between two rows of tall evergreens and come to a halt in front of a low, harshly lit building. They ask him to get out.

Cars are parked everywhere. Dozing chauffeurs sit in those closest to him. Some figures stagger about in the distance. Light and the din of voices flows from the open windows. A dignified fellow in a flawlessly tailored suit walks towards him. He stops in front of him. 'How was the ride, sir?'

He thanks him for asking. The man motions Fuka to follow him. They enter a hall, with several leather armchairs in its centre. The panelled walls are conspicuously bare, and the only other objects in the room are several glass cases, some filled with water, others with sand from which twisted branches and exotic plants protrude. 'Could I trouble you to sit down here for a moment?' the man says.

In one of the glass cases he can see the brown-and-black body of a snake. He gets up, but then, fearing he might be disrupting some kind of protocol, sits down again. What commitments does a man make when he accepts help? Does he surrender his freedom, or at least his independence? What value can work have when it is purchased with a loss of independence? What seems like an answer to his prayers might merely open the door to his downfall.

He is startled out of his thoughts by the sound of police sirens outside. He gets up and then sits down again. He can hear car doors slamming and the sound of voices. Then two uniformed men come in carrying a stretcher. He looks at them, but they pay no attention to him. They put the stretcher on the ground and wait.

The figure on the stretcher is motionless and almost entirely concealed by a blanket that reaches up to its mouth. Its head is bound in a white turban of bandages, its eyes are hidden behind dark glasses. Only its nose is visible, protruding sharply from its face. Fuka is gripped by anxiety as he stares at this strange creature.

Again, the man who seems to be a master of ceremonies appears. 'The president is ready to receive you.' Fuka gets up. The two uniformed men pick up the stretcher. They walk through several adjoining salons, where a reception must recently have taken place. Tables are scattered with empty glasses and dirty plates; scraps of food are drying out on large platters; swarms of flies circle over bits of caviar, chunks of ham in aspic, the crumbled wreckage of slabs of liver pâté, half-eaten pieces of chicken and turkey.

The last room he enters is full of people talking loudly. The moment he enters, the conversation dies. Deeply embarrassed, he looks around. He notices that there are chairs with high backs set up in a square, and that in the middle of this square is a magnificent armchair, almost a throne, which seems out of place here. It has gilded legs and a wooden back topped by a magnificent crown of carved wood set with diamonds. An old man in a black robe sits huddled in the chair.

At first he's not sure it *is* the president, for he has never seen him dressed like this. But that rather stocky figure, those grey eyes, those thick glasses, those fleshy lips, all undoubtedly belong to the head of state.

Why have they invited him here in the middle of the

night, with so many drunken guests around? He recognizes some from their pictures in the paper. He also recognizes the enormous black man trying to look dignified in a chair beside the throne: he is an official guest here on a state visit. The mystery deepens. What's going on? Will they bring him a camera and order him to film some insane midnight audience? An audience with whom?

With himself.

At that moment, a dwarfish little man pops up behind the president, as if from nowhere. He has enormous ears set so high on his skull they look like horns. He whispers something to the president. Fuka cannot hear the individual words, but he thinks he hears his own name and the word 'terrorist'. The face of the old man lights up in recognition. He opens his mouth as if to smile, and nods to him: 'Well, at last. Come forward!'

Because the words are obviously directed at him, Fuka approaches the throne. The men with the stretcher push in behind him. The old man watches them. When they place the stretcher at his feet, something in his stiff face moves, a barely perceptible grimace, or perhaps an expression of satisfaction.

Fuka doesn't know whether or not he is permitted to say anything, since he hasn't been spoken to, and in any case he doesn't know what he'd say even if he could, so he merely bows. The black man examines him with interest.

'Well now, my boy,' says the old man, speaking down to him from his throne. 'You submitted your appeal and here you are. With a stroke of the pen, I could have sent you to a place from which you would never return. But you're to have another chance, and you're here to explain yourself. So, what do you say? How do you wish to defend yourself?'

The old man tries to fix his eyes on him, but can't. They keep shifting, seeming to fade and then re-emerge from some inner depths. They are moist, filled with tears. 'You are silent. But then, when you raised your hand in anger, what then? You didn't hesitate then, you killed.'

Fuka is flabbergasted, and can only shake his head. The little man with the big ears steps forward and whispers something in the old man's ear. The old man nods. His eyes now appear to turn completely inward, searching for something in the depths. Then, aloud, he says something perhaps meant for himself, perhaps for the adviser or perhaps for everyone else: 'It doesn't matter. It doesn't matter. The one about the snakes, I remember, yes, I remember. You delighted us all. Do you have children?'

He shakes his head.

'And a wife?'

He doesn't have a wife, not really.

'So why, who do you do it for?' asks the man on the throne, and Fuka's astonishment is now shared by everyone present. No one says a word, except for the slender interpreter, who leans over and whispers something to the black statesman in a semi-audible voice.

'I know what you all want.' The powerful old man is now speaking to the rest and has lost interest in Fuka. 'You want clemency, you want freedom and power, but for what purpose? So that you can evade your responsibilities. So that you can abandon the ship, which I, with all my powers, am still . . . What do you think? Do you think I don't know, that I can't see, that I can't hear what you're rustling in your pockets, what you're clutching in your fingers, what you're whispering among yourselves? Who will dare to say that this is not so? Responsibilities!' he shouts. 'Responsibilities must be borne. Like me, like those wretched victims, who call out to me with piteous cries.' His glance shifts to his feet, where the stretcher is resting, but then immediately turns inward again. 'And they ask me to put an end to this, once and for all. No more special considerations!'

Absolute silence descends on the room like a curtain.

'I am the one who grants clemency here,' he bellows. 'And I'm the only one who knows, who acknowledges, my own responsibilities. And I will fulfil them. Let anyone who thinks he can stop me from . . . with a single stroke of the pen . . . ' And the head of state stands up, the black robe billowing around him. 'Who dares? No one? Good. Once again then, let everyone see, let everyone take note, that again and for the last time, as it once was, and is today, may you receive what you request! I grant you clemency. The executioner may leave!' He stretches his arms toward Fuka as if to bless him, then he takes a large step to avoid the stretcher and, while someone applauds, he disappears into the adjoining room. Everyone pushes in after him, while the two men in uniform lift the stretcher holding someone who may or may not be dead and carry it out.

They can carry the dead away, Fuka thinks, but death will always be here, and all he will take away from this place is death's caress. He knows that he could and should leave, but he is transfixed, staring at the bare wall as though intoxicated, until the master of ceremonies appears and announces: 'The audience is over. Allow me to congratulate you, sir.'

CHAPTER FOUR

1

THE COBBLESTONES WERE radiating heat and seemed to be shifting under Pavel's feet. This was happening to him more and more lately. Either he was drinking too much, or it took less than it used to.

He stopped in front of a small bar. From a distance he could hear the sound of a loudspeaker, but the words were incomprehensible. They could have been in Spanish. Maybe any moment now a small child's hand would press a wilted flower on him, or from the bar a dark-eyed mestiza would beckon him with a nod. He was thirsty. He looked through the open door into the bar, but it was so crowded he did not go in. Everyone was drinking more these days.

As he approached the lower part of the square he began to make out individual words. He was in no hurry to see who the speaker was. They no longer sent him out to cover demonstrations; he'd done all that back when the police were still beating the participants. It would probably not be a good thing if those who had once been beaten were to see him behind a camera again.

The invisible speaker was warning against the new rulers who had cleverly disguised themselves as people who once opposed the old ones. We all know, he said to his audience, that ideals were the furthest thing from their minds. All they wanted was power.

The distant crowd applauded. He would not have applauded. Everything was more complicated than any speech could describe, and even in this partisan crowd there were certainly a good number of the very people the speaker was talking about.

Recently he'd begun to think that without even leaving the country he'd become an alien. It wasn't that all the familiar faces had disappeared; it was that from behind those faces different people had appeared. Butterflies had emerged from their unsightly cocoons and, with growing astonishment at their new appearance, were looking around for places to alight.

Even in the new advertising company of which he was part owner, he was surrounded by such aliens, apart from Sokol, of course. They smiled at him and talked about deals. They expressed confidence in his ideas though they'd never seen a single one of his films. They simply smelled business. The warehouse they had bought to turn into a studio stank not only of old hides but also of this strangeness. He wandered through the gloomy space and thought about how many sections they needed and where the dividers should go, where to put the lights and how to make the acoustics work, but he couldn't make any decisions and went out for a drink instead. When he got to Eva's that evening, she began screaming at him. He was a disgusting drunk, he would come to a bad end, she no longer wanted anything to do with him.

He said he could understood that. He drank because he didn't want anything to do with himself either.

'What kind of nonsense is that?'

'That's something you'll never understand.'

'I know. As far as you're concerned I'm just a stupid cow who doesn't understand anything, but at least I don't drink like a fish.'

What could he say to her? She'd changed too. She no longer had anything in common with the past when she would come to him and want to make love to him.

'I thought you would finally stop drinking now.'

'Why now?'

'Because in those days it seemed to me there was

always something preying on your mind.'

'And what exactly did you think was preying on my mind?'

'Not being able to work the way you wanted to.'

'And you think I can work the way I want now?'

'Can't you?'

What could he say to her? Perhaps they would let him go on working, but his days were probably numbered. They were certainly going to watch him closely. Can you do what you want when you're being watched closely? And perhaps he didn't even know what he wanted. Perhaps he was his own worst enemy.

'You'll never sort anything out this way.'

She, on the other hand, had found a solution to her problems. She had decided to go back to her former husband. He at least cared for her; to him she was not just a woman to sleep with twice a week. It would be better for Robin as well. Kučera was his father, after all. She told Pavel that she wanted him to leave, but she wept as she said it. She wept because he had disappointed her, because she had wasted so much time with him, because he'd never expressed any gratitude to her. Sleeping with her twice a week had been all she was good for.

She wept even though her former husband would inherit a factory and almost certainly give her the money to buy a shop. Then she could believe that she was happy.

He should go back to Albina. If only he could. If only she existed. So instead, he went to see his mother, who still recognized him, though she sometimes confused him with his father.

He was a stranger, an alien. One of the many who were coming here to pillage, to set up in business, or merely as observers of the changing scene. Even the camera he still dragged around with him was a sign of his alien, observer status, a status that could not distinguish between what was essential and what was not, in which, for the most part, it was impossible to get excited about anything, regardless of the occasional need to pretend excitement. Indeed, it was with a growing coolness that he had recently filmed exhibitions, theatre rehearsals, interviews with artists and sessions in parliament, as well as the faces of new politicians. Once, he even filmed an address by the new president. This president had only one thing in common with his predecessor, and thus with Pavel as well: he had spent several years in prison. The new politicians had very little in common with the old ones, at least so far. Yet it was not his job to investigate what they were really like, but merely to capture their image, their gestures and their mimicry. Now and then he couldn't resist the occasional malicious close-up of twitching fingers that testified to insecurity, or some clumsiness of dress. He didn't do this to express an opinion, but merely to relieve the monotony and, unlike before, no one criticized him for doing this or cut them out of the broadcast. Was he unconsciously trying to give his new bosses an excuse for considering him unreliable? Or was he merely trying to persuade himself that this was now possible, that they had accepted him despite his recent past?

After work, he would drive to the still-unfinished studio and film mindless sequences in which beautiful models praised detergents they never used, new magazines that they'd never read and foreign cars they would love to drive but couldn't yet afford. They had plenty of commissions, and models as well. Sokol was convinced the models would love to get into riskier, more erotic things than what they had done so far, but Pavel felt that he had already sunk about as low as he was willing to sink.

They called their company Fusorek. Sokol claimed it sounded Japanese and would therefore evoke reliability. Pavel didn't care one way or the other.

At last he saw the speaker. A gaunt old man on an improvised platform was talking with great passion about how he had spent more than ten years in a prison camp, convicted on a trumped-up charge. The judge who had sentenced him was still on the bench today. What kind of justice, he asked, is meted out by those who once defiled the very name of justice? What kind of redress can we expect in a society where most of those who had a hand in the former crimes remain in their jobs? The revolution is not over, much is still to be done; it will not be complete until we cut out the ulcers that continue to eat away at the body politic.

He saw Little Ivens, who was filming the demonstration.

He was making a short about how people participated in the former crimes, a report on how they were an ulcer that needed cutting. His short will be so good that it will reap praise from those who hold the scalpel in their hands.

2

HIS MOTHER WAS lying on the bed with all her clothes on. She'd removed only her shoes. She didn't hear him when he came in.

'Mother!'

'Who's that?'

'It's me.'

'You, Pavel? Where have you been all this time?'

'I had work to do.'

'You're always so busy.' She closed her eyes again. 'And I'm here all alone.'

'Did you sleep?'

'Me? I haven't slept a wink. It's been at least a month, or a year; I don't remember when I last slept.'

He stood in the doorway. The room had not been aired for a long time: his mother was afraid of fresh air.

'Why don't you sit down?'

'Aren't you hungry?' he asked.

'No. That person was here again. Yesterday. He gave me food.'

'What did you have?'

'I don't know,' said his mother. 'I don't remember. I can't remember anything any more. Go on, sit down, but not in that armchair.'

'Why not?'

'There are worms in it.'

'Oh, Mother!'

'I saw them.'

'You must have been dreaming.'

'No, yesterday when that fellow was here to see me,

that do-gooder, he saw them too. He said the armchair should be thrown out.'

'I'll sit on this chair over here.'

His mother reached for the comb that lay on the bedside table and ran it through her thin hair. Recently, this had been practically her only activity. Step by step, reality was receding from her. She was even losing the power of speech and sometimes sought in vain for the most ordinary words. She put the comb down and closed her eyes.

After a while he had made up his mind to get Albina's address. She had moved to a small town and was working in an old people's home. It was comforting to know where he could find her if he wanted to see her. But he never went to visit and he never wrote to her.

Then he was filming a meeting in a large arms factory. When the work was done, he realized that he was close to the town where she lived, and that he could pass through it on his way back to the city without making a detour. The old people's home was situated in a small baroque château on the edge of town. He could have gone in and asked for her, but couldn't bring himself to do it. Next to the château was a park, so he went for a walk.

It was a warm, sunny autumn day and old men and women were sitting on the benches dressed in tracksuits and tartan slippers, their faces turned to the low sun. He found an empty bench, pulled a newspaper out of his pocket and pretended to read.

He didn't know whether Albina was on duty or even whether she was still working here. He should ask. Any one of these old people would have been glad to help. But instead, he sat and waited.

Then he saw her. She appeared in the rear gateway of the château pushing a wheelchair in which sat an old woman wrapped in a brightly coloured blanket. He recognized her petite figure at once, though her features were still obscured by the distance between them. She was walking along the pathway that would bring her to him. Was it an omen? She would certainly have said so.

He felt uncertain, then excited, as though he were waiting for a romantic encounter.

But she didn't come all the way to him. Instead she sat down on a bench and parked the wheelchair beside her. She bent over the old woman, rearranged her blanket and said something to her, but he was still too far away to hear her voice. Then she stood up straight and looked towards the roof of the old house, from which a flock of crows had just taken flight. She didn't glance in his direction at all. Was this an omen, the fact that she didn't even sense his presence, that nothing compelled her to turn in his direction so that she might see him? She would certainly have said so.

He could have walked over and spoken to her! 'Albina, I can't forget you. You are my only hope.'

But he didn't move, merely waited and watched her, and even at that distance he began to distinguish her features, still the same, still alluring. Occasionally an old man or an old woman would walk past and seem to greet her, because she always nodded her head, and he was certain that he recognized her familiar smile.

He had no idea how long they sat there, separated by no more than a few dozen paces. Then she got up, turned her back to him and pushed the wheelchair away in the opposite direction. He waited on his bench a while longer but he knew that he wouldn't see her again, that she would not return.

'Why are you always so silent?' said his mother suddenly. She reached again for her comb and ran it through her hair.

'What is there to talk about?'

'How should I know?'

'What are you interested in?'

'I'm interested in everything. In what you're doing.'

'Eva and I have split up.'

'Is she the one you found in the woods?'

'In the woods?'

'Well—you decided you'd run away from your mother, you went to the woods and that's where you found that German woman. Never a thought for me.'

He said nothing.

'Then you came and started doing—what do you call them?—pictures.'

'Films?'

'Yes, about that big do-gooder.'

'You mean the president?'

'Yes! And about those things that crawl. Is he still alive?'

'Who?'

'That fellow. Mr Do-good.'

'He's alive but he's not president any more.'

'I don't understand that.'

'There's another president now.'

'I don't understand, that he is and that he isn't any more. What are you going to do now that he isn't?'

'I'm going to make films.'

'I don't know—I don't know if you will or not, but I love you all the same, Pavel . . . you're my . . . what exactly are you? . . . my . . . ?'

'Your son.'

'I thought you were my Good Samaritan. And you were my husband before. Or maybe not. What am I? Your . . . ?'

'You're my mother.'

'Oh, go on,' she laughed. 'That was a long time ago.'

She combed her hair and then closed her eyes. 'I feel like eating something,' she said. 'I haven't eaten for days.'

'I'll make you some mashed potatoes.'

'You're going to make me mashed potatoes? You're not going to run away from me, into the forest? You're a good boy, Pavel. I'm fond of you.'

He went into the kitchen and took several potatoes out of the pantry. There were various things in the kitchen left over from the commercial shoots. Chewing-gum, different slicers and a set of supposedly ever-sharp knives. Using one of these, he peeled the potatoes and put them on the stove. He could have gone back in to his mother, but his conversation with her had exhausted him. He preferred to sit in the dark kitchen and watch the blue gas-flame.

A few days before, Robin had come to see him. He brought along the dog, and a large bag containing several neatly ironed shirts and his pyjamas. 'This is from Mum,' said the boy. 'She says you might need them.'

'Thanks.'

Argus rubbed up against him, then stood on his hind

legs, put his paws on his chest and licked his face.

'He misses you,' said Robin. 'He waits for you every day.'

He nodded. He had always got on better with dogs than people. Or rather, they got along better with him. He didn't like attributing human qualities to animals, but at least they certainly didn't try to own people, or punish them for being less than perfect.

The boy hesitated for a moment. 'Don't be angry with Mum,' he said. 'She means well. She thinks that I should be with my father.'

'I'm not angry with her.'

'You were always good to me,' said the boy. 'Honest. I feel bad that I might not see you again.'

'You can always come and visit me if you want to.'

'Thanks! But maybe they wouldn't like it.'

'I'm sure we'll see each other again.' He felt he should say something more, but instead he merely asked, 'Things going well at school?'

'It's OK.' Suddenly he perked up. 'School was always a pile of crap, but now they're teaching us things that weren't in the old textbooks. And we don't have to call the teachers "Comrade" any more.'

'Is that better?'

'I'll say!'

He rumpled Robin's hair and then gave him a fistful of chewing-gum before he left. He would probably never see him again.

His own son had never been born, and he'd lost his substitute son. He was surrounded by total strangers, and his mother barely recognized him.

He drained the potatoes, added milk and mashed them. Then he fried some eggs and put them on the plate with the mashed potatoes.

His mother had fallen asleep again. Her sunken cheeks were yellowish-grey and they puffed up slightly with each breath she took. The sound of feeble snoring came from her chapped lips.

He put the plate on the bedside table. 'Here's your food, Mother.'

She didn't move.

He spoke to her again, louder this time, and then he touched her shoulder with his hand. 'Mother!'

The doctor arrived in less than half an hour. She took his mother's pulse and blood pressure and looked under her eyelids. Then she sat down at the table and asked him a few questions, quickly jotting down his answers. 'We're taking your mother to the hospital. Here's an ambulance voucher. But I'm afraid that there's not a lot that can be done.'

'You think not?'

'She's eighty years old.'

'She hasn't been very well lately,' he said. 'Life was pretty much a burden to her.'

The doctor left. He called the ambulance, then sat in the armchair and looked at his mother. She was still breathing regularly, and her head rested on the pillow at an odd angle. He got up, ran the comb through her thin hair and stroked her forehead.

What was death?

You live for as long as you still see some meaning in being alive. You can live less than your allotted time, but not longer. It's not important whether you're still breathing or not.

Death is the moment a person, as an alien, falls among aliens and they surround him like a clinging layer of damp earth.

He suddenly felt the full weight of his mother's loneliness. He'd been with her so little in recent weeks and months, and hadn't stayed long even when he came to visit her, not even when he slept in her flat. And now, at this moment, he would have liked to make it up to her, but as usual he came to that realization when it was too late.

3

BEFORE HE SET out for the castle, he stopped in the little shop in the village. It was now in private hands, and offered several different kinds of wine and chocolate. At the castle, he learned that Alice had moved away two months ago. It might have occurred to him that she would not have stayed there by herself after Peter had gone.

Fortunately she had moved to a neighbouring town, where the local authorities had found her a flat. They desperately needed a nurse for their health centre. 'Nurses are leaving for abroad in droves,' the new custodian told him. 'They can make five times as much as they do here.'

It was evening by the time he reached the small house where she lived. A window on the second floor opened when he rang. 'Pavel, is that you?' She ran down, hugged him and held her face up to be kissed. Perhaps she was really glad to see him.

Her new flat was small and modestly furnished.

'I hear you're working again,' he said.

'Yes. The children are bigger, I have to make a living and I needed somewhere to live.'

'Are you enjoying it?'

'There's plenty to do. And life is interesting now,' she said, avoiding a direct answer. She took him into a small room with a couch, an armchair, a table and some shelves on the wall. Even with its meagre furnishings, the room seemed crowded. Some geraniums were blooming in a window-box. 'And what are you doing? Are you still working in television?'

'I'm about to leave,' he said. 'I've left Eva, and my mother died last month.'

'I'm sorry to hear that.'

'It was for the best.'

'That's too many things all at once. I want you to tell me all about everything, if you're not in a hurry.'

'No, I was only in a hurry to get here, to see you.'

'I still have to put the baby to bed. The others are fine on their own. Then we'll have time for ourselves.'

He would have liked to go with her, but would probably have been in her way.

There were several books on the shelves. A concise medical dictionary, nursing-school texts.

Haemorrhagai cerebri, brain haemorrhage.

Respiratio agonalis, terminal respiratory distress.

There was also an anthology of love poetry.

The geraniums gave off a faint, musty smell. He felt as

though he were suffocating. He stood up and opened the window wide and then went and opened the door slightly. As he did so, he caught a glimpse of her leaning over a small fair-haired child in the bathroom. Although she had had three children, her figure was still girlish.

She noticed him looking at her. 'Don't stare at me. My hair's a mess and I'm wearing these awful old clothes.'

'You look fine to me.'

She laughed, lifted the little boy to the floor and closed the door.

The fourth child, or really the first—his son—had never been born.

There was a newspaper lying on the table. He picked it up but couldn't concentrate on the headlines. It shook in his hands. He put it down and held out his fingers. Either I'm drinking too much, or I'm overexcited at the thought of being here alone with her.

Finally she came back, wearing a pale blue dress with a handmade lace collar. 'The collar was my grandmother's,' she said when she saw that he was looking intently at her.

'I'm not looking at the collar, I'm looking at you. You've changed so little. But you're more beautiful than you seemed then.'

'Thank you. You're flattering me, but it won't get you anywhere because I don't believe you.'

The children were either asleep or staying quiet. She spread a cloth on the table and put a bowl of apples on it. Then she brought in some sandwiches and a bottle of wine. She smiled at him but said nothing, and suddenly he couldn't bring himself to speak either.

Finally, she asked, 'How did your mother die?'

'In her sleep. She just fell asleep and never woke up. It was a stroke.'

'She had a nice death, if death can be nice.'

'When I was in Mexico, I asked an Indian how old he was and he said: soon it will be sixty-five years ago that I began to die. I didn't understand what he meant. He said that was how everyone there expresses his age. A person begins to die the moment he is born.' His voice sounded unnatural. He wasn't able to control the tremor in it. He reached for a glass and poured some wine for himself and for her.

'One day you'll see your mother again,' she said.

'Do you believe that? Where would all those who have ever died fit?'

'Into a space as small as one of those apples. Souls don't need space, and death can't be the end of everything.'

He wanted to object that everything not only could, but must, come to an end, that even the stars would one day go out, that only time would last for eternity. But he hadn't come here to argue with her about everlasting life.

'You know, you always were a bit spoilt. Your mother did everything for you,' she said.

'She didn't really,' he objected.

'You phoned me one evening and said there was something wrong with your heart. But your heart was all right, it was just that you'd overeaten.'

'My mother was in a spa at the time. I felt sad and lonely and I wanted you to come over, so I invented a pain in my chest.'

'You recovered pretty quickly, as I recall.' She laughed.

It had all happened too long ago. Twenty years ago. He shouldn't forget that. 'What about you?' he asked. 'Don't you ever feel sad and lonely?'

She became defensive. 'Everyone feels sad and lonely sometimes. But I'm alive. I'd be quite happy if . . . ' She shrugged her shoulders. 'If I only had a little more time. So many things are happening now, and I have the feeling that they're passing me by because my work . . . Illnesses, they're always the same. But what's happening now can never be repeated.'

'Nothing can ever be repeated.'

'Yes, but before it often seemed to me that one day was just like another. Now it's different.'

'Do you think it's really all that different now?'

'Doesn't it seem so to you?'

'Well, maybe it's just a new version of the old war. Over who keeps their job and who doesn't and who gets the most out of it.'

'You haven't changed, Pavel. You always see the worst side of everything. I happen to think that people have changed for the better. They have here at least, I don't know about where you work. Maybe you've rubbed someone the wrong way?'

'No. I've only rubbed myself the wrong way.'

'You've been doing that all your life.'

'Does anyone know how to live the way he'd like?'

'You're right. I'm no better. I believed—for the children's sake, not mine—that what happened to so many marriages would never happen to us.'

'It couldn't have been your fault.'

'I don't know. I racked my brains for a long time trying to work out whose fault it was. Then I said to myself that I can't be the judge, and that it's not so important anyway. The important thing is that it happened. Something I hadn't expected. I don't think Peter expected it either. You often do things you don't want to do, or at least you end up somewhere you never wanted to be.'

'Maybe he'll come back.'

'He won't come back, and even if he did I wouldn't want him to.'

'Why did it happen?'

She shrugged. 'Maybe it was the times we lived in that did it. He couldn't do what he wanted to do and live the way he wanted to live. Or perhaps it was already in him. Some discontent. Maybe it was a need to destroy what he loved. Maybe I wasn't interesting enough for him. Or maybe he just fell in love.' She got up and walked over to the window so he wouldn't see the tears in her eyes.

'He sometimes comes to visit,' she said. 'Actually, he comes to see the children. He tells me what he's doing, of course, but he's never mentioned you. He never told me that you were going to leave.'

'Several of us have set up a studio and we're going to make our own films. We're going to be more free to do what we want.'

'Are you really going to make your own films?'

Her question took him aback. He ought to let her think so, to keep alive the notion that he was acting more freely. But he told her the truth. 'So far we're only making commercials.'

'Ads? You can't be serious.' She came back to the table, apparently relieved that they were no longer talking about her.

'To make an independent film that no one is going to mess around with I need money. Advertising is a way of making money.'

'I suppose I just don't understand. I thought that when the moment came and you were able . . . that you'd do something really wonderful.'

'Did you really think that?'

'Didn't you think that too?'

'Almost everyone thinks that of themselves. There's nothing easier than persuading yourself you could really do something if you tried, as long as you know that they'll never give you the chance. The system never allowed you to win, and so it saved you from defeat as well.'

'You told me you were writing a screenplay.'

'Yes.'

'Have you written it?'

'Yes.'

'What's it called?'

'Waiting for the Dark, Waiting for the Light.'

'Waiting for the Dark?' she repeated.

'That's it.'

'And *Waiting for the Light*. What are you waiting for now?'

'It made sense to make the film when it couldn't be made. It doesn't make sense now.'

'If you've written a good screenplay, why wouldn't it make sense now?'

'I don't know whether it's any good or not. I don't know whether you'd like it. Probably not. It's mad.'

'I like madness.'

'I wrote it as a reaction against what I was doing. It was a kind of escape.'

'Yes,' she said. 'You've always tried to escape. Do you remember you promised to take me with you to Mexico? It was like promising me a trip to the moon. When you finally got there, you didn't even send me a postcard.'

'But I thought of you when I was there.'

'I'm supposed to believe you?'

'In a big colourful market-place near Tula I bought a turquoise bracelet to give to you some day when we saw each other again, but then I thought that it wouldn't be appropriate. I still have it at home.'

'Didn't you give it to Eva?'

'It was for you.'

'Why did you leave Eva?' she said, ignoring his reassurance.

'It hadn't been great between us for some time. My drinking upset her.'

'I don't blame her a bit.'

'One of the reasons I drank was because I didn't have anyone to love.'

'You always have an explanation for everything.'

'We were together out of necessity, and the necessity ended. At least for her. She went back to her husband.'

'Well, good for her.' He thought there was a note of grumpiness in her voice, perhaps a touch of jealousy, and it encouraged him.

'Did you let her read your screenplay?' she asked quickly, as though she wanted to avoid the topic of possible reconciliations.

'No, I haven't let anyone read it. It was too personal to let anyone read it, at least anyone close to me.'

'Personal? Was it about her?'

He shrugged his shoulders.

'Or about you?'

'It was just personal.'

'But there's nothing about me in it?'

He said nothing.

'Who's waiting for the dark and who's waiting for the light?'

'The heroine is waiting for something the hero is unable to give her. It's also about a lot of other things.'

'You're intriguing me. What's the heroine's name?'

'That's not important. Her name is Albina,' he said. 'It's not about you. I invented her. But I invented her in a way that reminds me a little of you.'

'Why me?'

'I think you can probably guess.'

'It seems strange, with your profession. You're sur-
rounded by so many women. Or did you write it because
of the child? Tell me, is there something about that in it
too?'

'It's not about us. I tell you it's not about us. I changed
everything.'

'But you can't change that.'

'You can change anything in a film.' Then he said
quietly, 'As a matter of fact there is something about the
child in it.'

'So am I such a terrible murderer that you're afraid to
tell me right out what it is you really want to make the film
about?'

'On the contrary.'

'What does that mean: on the contrary?'

'You would know, if you read it, that you are the only
person on earth that I still care about.'

'Now you're starting to get really personal.'

'That's why I've come.'

'Your mother died, you've separated from Eva and
you've come to tell me that I'm the only person you have
left?'

'Yes.'

'It's a shame you left it so late, Pavel. In the meantime, I
got married and had three children.'

'I don't have any, Alice.'

'But you could have had.'

'You still haven't forgiven me for that?'

'I forgave you long ago. It was my fault as much as it
was yours.'

'No. I persuaded you to do it. A child didn't seem to fit
into our plans. You weren't even seventeen, and I . . . well,
I thought I had to do a lot of things before I could allow
myself the luxury of being a father. Now I know it was the
worst thing I've ever done in my life. Everything else fol-
lowed from that.'

'What can I say to you, Pavel?'

'If there was some way I could make up for it.'

'You can't make up for it, Pavel. You can't bring it back

to life. It's dead. We had it killed before it was born.'

'I'd like to have a child with you, Alice.'

'It's too late, Pavel.'

'I thought—do you remember how we last met during that big demonstration, and we went into that little bar and the television was on . . . '

'Of course I remember.'

'You kissed me out of the blue, and it seemed . . . it seemed that we were as close then as we were all those years ago.'

'It was the moment that did it, Pavel, the time. We were all close in those days.'

'Is that time over now?'

'A time like that can't last for very long.'

'So it's too late, Ali?'

'I can't start all over again with you. I don't know if I could live with someone else, but I do know that the two of us can't begin again. You said yourself that nothing can repeat itself.'

'Exactly. I wouldn't want to repeat anything.'

'You'd want to start something completely different?'

He nodded.

'That's impossible. We're not completely different. You're sad and lonely, maybe too sad and lonely. And I really feel sorry for you, Pavel. But that's not enough.' She leaned over and stroked his hair. The way she caressed her children.

4

THEIR FIRM, WITH a name that might have sounded Japanese to anyone not in the know, had been going for a year. The company's accountant, one of the many aliens who had forced their way into his life, suggested that they celebrate the anniversary with a reception to which they would invite as many entrepreneurs—that is potential customers— as possible. The reception, of course, had to take place in one of the top hotels.

Pavel had no objections. He didn't get involved in the

business side of things. It didn't interest him. He tried to do his job well, even to the point of watching pre-war film advertisements in the archives. They seemed wittier than present-day commercials. But he did this only out of professional habit; the work did not satisfy him, nor did he enjoy it. But how else was he to spend his time?

When he drank a little more than he should, his head would ache, and he would feel, more frequently now, an unpleasant pressure in his chest. He was afraid of solitude, yet found himself alone more and more often. The blank spaces in his life that could not be filled were increasing, spaces left by his mother, by Albina and even by Eva, although he could fill that particular blank any time he felt like it. Writing his screenplay occupied his time, but unfortunately he had only two or three final scenes left to write. He put off working on them; what would he do when he had finished?

He bought a new Mercedes coupé even though he had to sell a baroque table from his cottage to raise the money. Sokol was furious; he considered their private assets part of the firm's common property. His plan was to buy a well-located shop when the state began auctioning them off, where he would open a large electronics store. Didn't Pavel understand that there would be a high reserve price, and that other interested parties would have to be bribed to stay out of the bidding? Where would the money for that come from if he squandered what he had on cars?

But he didn't need a big store. He needed a new car.

'What for?'

'For life.'

'You don't understand. Either the firm grows or it dies.'

'I've been dying for forty-eight years now.'

The car was vermilion. Everything was automatic, and the speedometer showed speeds of up to three hundred kilometres an hour.

He drove his new car to the reception, arriving as late as he could. There were more familiar faces here than he expected, faces he remembered from past meetings and conferences. These faces had ruled over ministries, press agencies, factories, personnel departments, the television network and him. Halama was there. He now owned a private radio station that broadcast the same hit songs he himself had so recently banned. He saw a poet with whom he'd once made a film about folk carvings of nativity scenes. The poet had gained official recognition by writing verses that expressed his love for women, the motherland and the Party. Now, anonymously, he wrote copy expressing his love of ever-sharp kitchen knives, ketchup and chewing-gum. Also, after a moment of uncertainty, Pavel recognized the good-looking strawberry-blonde who seemed to keep looking his way. He'd never known her name, but years ago he'd made love to her at a party near the explosives factory. He wondered if she had got back together with her husband, whose pockets had been filled with cheques from sheikhs and terrorists made out for amounts he could not even imagine. Even Little Ivens was here with a film crew to make a documentary about the new entrepreneurs. Little Ivens had now taken his place, but he had no reason to feel resentful about it because he had relinquished his job voluntarily.

He had no desire to be resentful about anyone.

He took a plate of sandwiches and as he did so he recalled his evening at the drama faculty. He remembered the room full of people sleeping on the floor, the girl who had offered him her blanket, the feeling of nearness to students he didn't know by name but who could easily have been his children. In the end, they had delivered handmade posters by car. What were the names of the two students who went with them? He couldn't remember, though he'd know them if he ever met them again. It hadn't occurred to him to invite the student who wanted to be a cameraman here. How could he, if he didn't know his name?

He felt an unexpected sense of uneasiness, as though he'd made a mistake and it had suddenly come back to haunt him.

He ought to have invited the student who could easily have been his son. It wouldn't have been so difficult to find out his name. But he might have felt embarrassed in front of him now.

He drank some cognac and went to look for Peter, whom he had invited. He found him in conversation with Halama.

That of course is the role of sons in the lives of their fathers—to remind them what they had to be ashamed of.

'I didn't know you knew each other,' he said, when he'd led Peter aside.

'Of course we do. A few years ago he tried to stop me from being a custodian.'

'Why?'

'He knew me from the faculty and considered me a subversive element.'

'And now he's talking to you?'

'Why shouldn't he talk to me? It's over and done with. And now he's your guest, just as I am. He's offering me a place in his production team because he doesn't think I'll be in television much longer.'

'Is that what he thinks? Nobody's going to fire you.'

'No one fired you either.'

'But I had reasons for leaving.'

'What were they? You always claimed you were waiting for freedom,' said Peter. 'It seems to me you could use it for something better than this.'

'Possibly, but I don't intend to do this for the rest of my life.'

'Here's hoping you're not just making excuses. But your decision is your affair. Maybe I'd have done the same thing in your place.'

But Peter wasn't in his place, and he had always acted differently. Or not always perhaps, but usually. With regard to Alice, they'd ended up the same. They should drink to that, drink to the fact that at least in something they had come to the same end.

'No one's throwing me out,' said Peter. 'But I probably won't be staying there much longer. I don't know people in broadcasting, and they don't know me. I was out of the picture for far too long. They don't think of me as someone who understands their business. I'm just someone who's been sent in to sort things out.'

'Do you feel unappreciated?'

'No, I feel alone.'

'And would you work for him, for Halama?'

Peter became animated. 'Never! Maybe I'll go back to being a castle custodian.'

'Back to Alice?'

'There are a lot of castles. In some cases, the former owners are getting them back. Maybe I'd get on with some of them.'

'What makes you think that?'

'They were out of things for a long time too.'

He laughed. 'You don't mean any of this seriously.'

The music began to play and he went to get another drink. No one is the same as they were, he thought. Nothing has stayed the same as it was.

Little Ivens stopped him. 'Would you like to say something on camera about your business, Pavel? So I can help my old buddies wipe out the competition?' He grinned at him as affably as he knew how.

'And how are things going for you?' Pavel asked.

'Oh, it's fine—you know how it is. The work's pretty much the same. There's a little more elbow-room but not all that much. You get so used to watching yourself, you don't overstep the mark.'

'But you don't have to watch yourself.'

'Maybe not,' he admitted, 'but like I say, it's in my blood. I'm always trying to satisfy the people who make the decisions. I think it's the same all over the world.'

Or perhaps, Pavel thought, the world around us *has* changed, and now we're trying to recreate it in its old form.

Again he noticed the strawberry-blonde. He wondered who had invited her here, and why. He went over to her, bowed slightly and asked her to dance. She nodded and looked at him curiously. 'Do we know each other?'

'We met some time ago. You told me about your husband and his travels.'

'These days anyone can travel.'

'You don't travel any more?'

She shook her head. 'My husband's gone into politics. He's working at the Ministry.'

Perhaps that was why she was here. 'Foreign Trade?' he asked.

'No, Privatization. But that's foreign trade too.' She laughed. Not a word about those cheques for unimaginable amounts. Either she'd made up with her husband, or she hadn't had as much to drink as she'd had the last time they met. He felt certain that large amounts of money were still changing hands under the table.

'Have you moved?'

'No, I have enough to do in . . . where I lived when we met.' Perhaps she'd managed to place him.

'Business?'

She looked at him warily. 'Something like that.' She said no more, as if she wanted to concentrate fully on the dance.

They'd barely finished dancing when Sokol came up to him and, with an apology, drew him aside. 'I'd like to introduce you to someone. This guy thinks erotic videos will sell very well. He has money, and if we are interested he'll come in with us.'

'You know I can't stand videos, even when they're not erotic.'

'Whatever. But you should meet him. It looks like a great business. And if we don't take him up on it, he'll go in with someone else.'

'I couldn't care less. I won't do it.'

'I'd like you to talk to him.'

'Here?'

'You know a better place? We don't have to commit ourselves.'

'I won't talk to him. I'm not in the mood, and I'd mess up the deal.'

'So you'll leave it up to me? Good. But I hope you won't suddenly get all unreasonable if I work something out with him.' He walked directly across to a young man with yellow hair tied in a short pony-tail. He had an earring and was wearing a purple jacket. He probably owned a massage parlour or something like that.

The strawberry-blonde was waiting for him. Would she make love to him again in an empty room? That wouldn't be possible here. They would have to go somewhere else. He didn't even know if she was here alone or not.

By now he was having trouble breathing, and the floor had begun to heave beneath him. It was time to leave. He looked at the woman, who had gone off to get a drink. He still didn't know her name. She was probably here by herself. He could always ask her. But he didn't feel like asking, not about that, not about anything. He didn't expect answers from anyone any more, not even from himself.

He wanted to leave by himself and go as far away as possible. Somewhere where he knew no one, where aliens were really aliens, a place where there were no people at all, only rocks and birds.

FILM

FUKA WALKS AROUND the food tables towards the exit. He passes the bar, where they are still serving drinks. He reaches out for a full glass, knocks it back, and continues on his way.

Black diplomatic limousines are parked outside waiting for the guests. The limousine that brought him is no longer there. He hurries past, trying not to see them, and looks up at the stars shining though the trees. When he walks through the gate and past the guard he almost breaks into a run. He hails a taxi. He should go to Ella's, but he now thinks of her as part of the bizarre world ruled over by that deranged old crackpot.

The sky above the rooftops is turning light by the time he gets back to the studio. He sits down in a chair and stares straight ahead. He can still see the old man, and the stretcher.

After a while he gets up, goes to the telephone and dials a number. 'It's me,' he says to Ella. 'I'm back.'

'Where are you calling from?'

'From my place.'

'Why didn't you come here?'

'I didn't want to wake you up.'

'What happened? What did he say to you?'

'Nothing. He granted me clemency.'

'Come on, tell me what happened.'

'Nothing,' he says. 'Nothing happened. He didn't know who I was. Maybe he doesn't even know who he is.'

'That's impossible! What do you mean, he granted you clemency?'

'Everything is possible. That's the only thing I learned. That's the only thing I understood. Anything can happen.'

He hangs up and rips the cord out of the wall. Then he goes to the cupboard, pulls out a box and riffles through the photographs until he finds Alina's picture. Her wistful face, her faint smile, looks at him lovingly as though trying to tell him something. But she will not grant him clemency.

Soon he's racing his sports car through the empty streets, and then along country roads. In a small town he pulls up in front of a snack bar, has a coffee, buys a sandwich and takes it back to the car. He's in a hurry. He drives out of the town, past a baroque manor house transformed into a refuge for elderly men and women abandoned by their families, past a park, a hospital, a brewery. He turns off the main road and stops at the corner of a street. He gets out, goes into a block of flats, checks the names until he finds the one he's looking for. The lift isn't working, so he runs up the stairs to the third floor and stops in front of the door to Alina's flat. He's just about to ring the bell when he notices the seal around the door. He stares at it in shock and then rings the bell of the neighbouring flat. The door is opened at once by a woman wearing a dressing-gown. She has obviously been watching him through the peep-hole.

'You've come to see her?' she asks him.

He nods.

'Are you a friend of hers?'

'What's happened to her?'

'You don't know? You're not from around here?'

'No. What happened to her?'

'That monster, the one who tried to shoot all those children in the bus at the border . . . he killed her.' The woman's voice catches. 'It happened last night. I saw her when they carried her out. No one knows why he did it or how he got inside. But they were after him, with dogs.

There was a lot of commotion, and then he jumped out of the window. Didn't kill himself. They took him off in an ambulance.'

'Is she really dead?' But he doesn't wait to hear her answer. He wants to preserve a fragment of hope. He thanks her and goes down the stairs.

By now it is daylight, and children are leaving for school.

He gets into his car, starts the engine, then turns it off again and lays his head on the steering-wheel. His shoulders begin to shake spasmodically.

Then he's driving again but he doesn't know where he's going. Perhaps he's not even driving, perhaps the car is driving itself. He has become a shadow. If the wind were to blow now, it would blow right through him the way it blows through a flat in which the doors and the windows have been left open, but the wind can't blow here. There's nothing here. He's driving through emptiness, utter emptiness, through nothing, through a white screen bisected by the taut black line of the horizon.

A red light begins blinking on the dashboard, the horizon wavers, the screen turns yellow and dissolves into long grass reflected in water.

He drives to the edge of a pond and stops.

The sun is high in the sky and billows of white fog roll over the mountain peaks.

He leaves everything in the car, his documents, his camera bag, his camera. He takes off the formal jacket he's still wearing from last night and pulls on the old black sweater he takes with him wherever he goes. He carefully locks the doors of the car and tosses the keys into the pond. A narrow pathway winds among the high brownish grass, which may be stalks of sargasso.

In front of him several bare, jagged cliffs rise abruptly to the sky. It is another country.

The sun beats down.

A flock of black ravens rises out of the grass and takes to the air. They look like black crosses floating in the sky.

The cliffs still seem far away, but it doesn't matter, he's in no hurry to get there, no hurry to get anywhere. He wipes sweat from his forehead. He feels thirsty, so he tears off a few stalks of grass and slowly chews them. They taste bitter, and he makes a face.

He comes to a stream. The water is shallow and transparent and seems clean. He takes a drink and continues walking up the path beside its bed. As the path rises more steeply the stream gets narrower, and the water roars and plunges into the depths.

He finds the source of the stream just below a stony peak. He takes another drink, then finds a wide flat stone, takes off his sweater, rolls it into a ball, lies down and places it under his head.

On the other side of the mountains, down below, he can pick out the rooftops of a distant village, and he sees smoke rising from a fire somewhere quite close, although he doesn't know where; he's in a completely alien place.

The sky is a deep mountain blue, with pure white clouds sailing across it. He'd once taken pictures of them. Hands and clouds.

He looks up to the emptiness above him.

The sun is still beating down. The water beside him ripples over the stones, and the wind whistles loudly among the rocks. Among those sounds, which intensify the silence, he suddenly hears a distant voice calling his name. He jumps up, leans over and looks down.

'Is that you, Ali?' Then he sees her, running up the narrow path. She stops, and looks up towards him.

'Should I come to you?' he asks, so quietly that surely she cannot hear him, but she does because she nods and spreads her arms wide, and he stands above the abyss and imagines that he is a bird, a black raven or a large bird of prey, a condor. He steps lightly over the edge of the cliff and glides in great circles into the depths.

EPILOGUE

WORK WAS OVER for the day. Lights were turned off. The slightly drunk model who had performed a sex act with an assigned partner put her clothes back on. She had a nice figure and her well-proportioned face was even pretty, as long as you weren't looking for evidence of intelligence in it. As she finished dressing, Pavel felt aroused by the sight of her.

'Would you like a ride home?' he asked her.

'That would be very kind of you, Mr Fuka.'

'You can call me Pavel.'

His new sports car was parked outside. He opened the door for her.

'My God, I've never been in one like this before.'

'Do you want to have supper?'

'If you're inviting me.'

He drove off. There was still some time left before evening, and he felt like going for a drive.

'Do you mind if we go out of town?'

'Why not! I'm free now, since we've finished.'

'Have you got your passport with you?'

'Passport? What do I need a passport for?'

'It's not that far to the border, and in this thing we'll be there in a little while.'

'You want to drive that far?'

'Maybe. We'll see.'

'I'd have to go home for it.'

'When I was your age,' he said, as they left the city, 'I desperately wanted to go abroad.'

'Of course, doesn't everyone?' Apparently she didn't understand why he was telling her this.

'But in those days it was impossible.'

'I just love shopping there. When I have the wherewithal.'

'If we stay there till tomorrow, you'll have the wherewithal.'

She half turned her head and then leaned over to him and kissed him. Warm air rushed through the open window. The countryside flashed by so quickly that individual objects became smudges.

She rested her head on his shoulder and sighed blissfully. After a while she said, 'I hope you don't think badly of me. I just took the job because they promised me a better part next time. What I really want to do is act.'

'Maybe it'll work out for you.'

'I wanted to go to drama school, but they wouldn't take me. I didn't have any contacts. Not even someone's father.'

'Lots of great actresses never went to drama school.'

'The worst is starting out. Before anyone notices you.'

She was probably thinking that this was her big chance, now that he'd noticed her.

When they were nearing the border, the road began to rise into the mountains. He drove on to a track leading into a field and stopped. 'Time for a break,' he announced. 'Shall we go for a little walk?'

'I'd rather drive.' But she got out of the car.

He took off his jacket and put on a sweater that he always carried with him. He took out his camera, carefully locked the door and stuck the keys in his trouser pocket.

'Are you going to take pictures of me?'

He shook his head. 'I don't want to leave anything inside.'

'Where are we going?'

'Nowhere in particular.'

The narrow pathway wound up to the top of a hill. It

was already twilight in the woods. He put his arm around her waist.

'I don't like walking uphill,' she said, panting. 'Let's go back now. Or we can stay here if you like.'

He found a grassy spot among the trees. He took off his sweater and laid it on the grass.

'Do you like it here?' she asked.

'I like you,' he said.

'I like you too.' She took off her skirt and laid it beside his sweater. When he took her in his arms, she gave a practised moan.

It was so dark now that he could hardly make out her features. Oddly enough, he couldn't remember them. She was such a complete stranger that if she had slipped out of his embrace at that moment and become another woman, he wouldn't have noticed.

When they had crossed the border, she said, 'There! Now you're abroad!'

'Yes.' He should have explained to her that he had lived and moved among foreigners for a long time now, but she wouldn't have understood, and wouldn't have been interested anyway.

They had dinner in a small hotel just over the border and took a room there for the night. She got drunk and fell asleep as soon as she lay down. He too was a little drunk. His stomach felt heavy, and every breath he took was accompanied by a stabbing pain in his chest.

He lay beside the stranger, stared into the emptiness and felt anxious. Sleep did not come, and he was sure that it never would. He had to do something, go somewhere, start something—or end something. He got up, though he knew he had nowhere to run to. He flung aside the curtain and looked out of the window. The dimly lit car park was full of cars. His red sports car seemed to have changed colour. He got dressed quickly, drank a glass of water in the bathroom and then slipped out of the door. The night air was fresh and smelled of jasmine. The stars were sparkling in a cloudless sky, and the hotel's neon sign glowed redly behind him. He was abroad, he was finally where he had once longed to be, and he had an expensive car and a mistress with him. He should feel some sense of satisfaction now, but what he noticed most was the pain in his chest and the emptiness above him.

He got into his car. He could hear the sounds of jazz coming from a nearby bar. He'd come back for the stranger in the morning. He started the car and drove out through the gates of the car park.

Wedding guests are crowding through the open gate. Fuka, tall and thin, has on a slightly worn black suit. Alina is clinging to him in a pale blue dress with a collar and cuffs of white lace. He kisses her, then lifts her up as gently as he can and carries her in his arms over the string that his friends have stretched across their path. The wedding guests form two lines, and as they walk between them to a coach hitched to a pair of sorrels, the guests shower them with flowers. The coachman in a top hat shakes the reins, and the coach sets off.

'Where are you taking me?' Alina says, still clinging to him.

'It doesn't matter. We'll be at home wherever we are.'

'My God,' she laughs, 'You must know where we're going to live.'

'I have nothing,' he says. 'But I've bought a big tent.'

'That's what we're going to live in?'

'Why not?'

'Yes, why not! I'm looking forward to your big tent.'

He thought that this might make a good beginning for his new screenplay.

It was only a short distance to the Autobahn, which was almost empty at this time of night. He sped through the alien countryside, and the faster he drove the greater his sense of relief.

Suddenly he saw an enormous tent pitched directly ahead of him in the middle of the road. In the light of his headlights he could see the red-and-white striped canvas. The horses whinnied impatiently. He braked slightly and at that moment his bride, no longer in pale blue but all in white, was beside him. 'Is that you, Ali?'

She presses close to him, embraces him and kisses him, and kisses him again.

Fortunately, the entrance to their dwelling opens wide. He drives through it, and the horses don't stop but plunge forwards with increasing frenzy.

He suddenly feels anxious and reaches beside him with his right hand, but his fingers close on a void. His bride has vanished. Perhaps she has been sucked up in a whirlwind. The countryside also seems to have vanished.

Nothing distracts him now, and he feels he can almost rise above the earth, rise above his own life as though it belonged to someone else.

What is life?

Which life is really my own?

Translator's Acknowledgements

I would like to thank Ivan Klíma for his trust and willingness to help clarify some of the inevitable ambiguities in the text; and Ursula Doyle for her sensitive reading and editing of the translation.

My deepest gratitude goes to Patricia Grant who, with her assistance, suggestions, enthusiasm and good humour, made it possible to finish the translation on schedule.

Paul Wilson, Toronto, August 1994

The Ultimate Intimacy

'A writer of enormous power and originality.' Patrick McGrath

'*The Ultimate Intimacy* is a quiet, intense study of a man who moves from a state of emotional neutrality to one of controlled complexity . . . Klíma skilfully catches the confusion, ambiguity and the stalemate strangling of the lives of his characters . . . [his] achievement remains his understanding of moral and emotional confusion and his ability to question these dilemmas.' Eileen Battersby, *Irish Times*

My Golden Trades

'Each of the six stories here is based on a job that the narrator, a banned writer, is forced to do for economic or psychic survival . . . Klíma gives us many melodies: a real and terrifying world, a caustic and philosophic commentary, and a transcendent imagination . . . some of the best stories I've ever read.' Carole Angier, *New Statesman & Society*

'A consistent celebration of man's freedom from the tyranny of circumstance . . . Klíma has turned the various humiliating trades which he was forced to practise into the purest artistic gold.' Michael Dibdin, *Independent on Sunday*

The Spirit of Prague

This collection of essays by one of Europe's most brilliant and humane novelists charts five critical decades in the history of Czechoslovakia.

'Ivan Klíma is one of the greatest writers of Czechoslovakia. He is as good as Milan Kundera, Josef Škvorecký, and Václav Havel.' *Daily Telegraph*

For further information about Granta Books
and a full list of titles, please write to us at

Granta Books

2/3 HANOVER YARD

NOEL ROAD

LONDON

N1 8BE

enclosing a stamped, addressed envelope

———————————

You can visit our website at

http://www.granta.com